Starting Social Work

Reflections of a Newly Qualified
Social Worker

Other books you may be interested in:

Anti-racism in Social Work Practice
Edited by Angie Bartoli   ISBN 978-1-909330-13-9

Modern Mental Health: Critical Perspectives on Psychiatric Practice
Edited by Steven Walker   ISBN 978-1-909330-53-5

Positive Social Work: The Essential Toolkit for NQSWs
By Julie Adams and Angie Sheard   ISBN 978-1-909330-05-4

Evidencing CPD – A Guide to Building Your Social Work Portfolio
By Daisy Bogg and Maggie Challis   ISBN 978-1-909330-25-2

Personal Safety for Social Workers and Health Professionals
By Brian Atkins   ISBN 978-1-909330-33-7

What's Your Problem? Making Sense of Social Problems and the Policy Process
By Stuart Connor   ISBN 978-1-909330-49-8

Titles are also available in a range of electronic formats. To order please go to our website www.criticalpublishing.com or contact our distributor NBN International, 10 Thornbury Road, Plymouth PL6 7PP, telephone 01752 202301 or email orders@nbninternational.com

Starting Social Work

Reflections of a Newly Qualified
Social Worker

 Rebecca Joy Novell

First published in 2014 by Critical Publishing Ltd.

British Library Cataloguing in Publication Data
A CIP record for this book is available from the British Library

ISBN: 978-1-909682-09-2

This book is also available in the following e-book formats:
Kindle ISBN: 978-1-909682-10-8
EPUB ISBN: 978-1-909682-11-5
Adobe e-book ISBN: 978-1-909682-12-2

Cover design by Greensplash Limited
Project Management by Out of House Publishing
Typeset by Newgen Imaging Systems
Printed and bound in Great Britain by TJ International

Critical Publishing
152 Chester Road
Northwich
CW8 4AL
www.criticalpublishing.com

MIX
Paper from
responsible sources
FSC
www.fsc.org   FSC® C013056

Dedication

Reid Finlay

The first few months of my Masters course in social work were somewhat overshadowed by how much I was struggling financially. I was several thousand pounds in debt, couldn't afford to pay rent and could only afford one meal a day. I was working every evening and weekend to try and earn enough to continue my course but I soon realised that I would not be able to sustain my lifestyle for two years. Anyone who has struggled with money will know the pervasive impact it has on your life. It is a source of constant worry, stress and sadness. I was very low for many weeks. Knowing how much I wanted to do social work, and knowing that I couldn't afford to, was heartbreaking.

One evening in late October, I remember clearly, I was sitting at a bus stop in the outer suburbs of Sheffield after another evening shift as a social carer. It was dark and cold and pouring down with rain. My bus was typically late. After 40 minutes of waiting I burst into tears. I remember literally sobbing in the street. Luckily there was no one around to see me as the pathetic mess I was. As I started to pull myself together, my Mum rang me. To this day I still believe that phone call was a miracle.

Mum knew I had been struggling with money and had rung to tell me that her Uncle Reid, who had met me twice as a young child, was willing to pay off all my debts, pay my rent for two years and provide me with a weekly income. Reid was willing to do all that because he knew from my Mum just how much I wanted to be a social worker. Unsurprisingly I reverted to uncontrollable sobbing.

Because of Reid, I was able to continue the course; and without the constant worry of lack of money. Reid gave me the two greatest academic years of my life. I spent every day learning how to help people to the best of my ability. He enabled me to spend my time concentrating on the thing I love most in the world.

I completed the course in July 2012 and graduated in January 2013. I was waiting until my Graduation Day to tell Reid exactly how much he had done for me; to tell him that completing this Masters and qualifying as a social worker is my proudest achievement to date; to tell him thank you.

I found out in October 2012, almost two years exactly since the miracle, that Reid passed away in the night. It was sudden but it was peaceful.

I am filled with incredible guilt and sadness that I did not tell Reid what he meant to me sooner. Reid barely knew me but was willing to give his money to see me fulfil my dream. My admiration for him is indescribable.

My Mum has told me that before he died, Reid put aside enough money for me to start a PhD. Something I desperately want to do but never in my wildest dreams thought I could afford.

I want you to know Reid, that because of you I spend every day trying to help some of the most vulnerable children in our society. With social work I have found my purpose in life. The work I do and the people I work with complete me.

I am devastated that the world no longer has you in it. My memories of you are as a kind and gentle man and I promise to work tirelessly to ensure that your generosity continues through me.

All I can really say (and what I should have said a long time ago) is *Thank you*.

Rest in peace, Reid.

CONTENTS

Meet the author

Rebecca Joy Novell

Rebecca Joy Novell is a Newly Qualified Social Worker (NQSW) working for a charity in Sheffield which works with homeless young people. She graduated from The University of Sheffield in 2012 with a Masters in social work. Rebecca has been involved with youth justice for five years in a variety of voluntary and paid roles, and is currently undertaking a PhD in Criminal Justice. She was recently elected to the Professional Assembly for The College of Social Work and regularly blogs for *The Guardian*'s Social Care Network.

Acknowledgements

The process of writing this book has made me realise just how lucky I am; I owe a lot of thanks to a lot of people. I would like to thank my parents, Emma Mulliner and everyone who took the time to proofread my ramblings. Thanks to Di for taking a chance on me. But I would also like to thank all those people who have carried me through the lowest moments in my life and have led me to this happy moment; Mum, Dad, Nanna, Reid, Miss Allen, the nine LGGS girls, G2, G1, Louise and Mr Leitch.

Thanks to my Godfather Brian who taught me to see the good in everyone. To Andy for being the best 'cornerman' I could ever ask for. To the women who continue to challenge and inspire me as a social worker: Nora and Nell. And to my partner, Rob, who has spent numerous evenings dealing with all my worries. While I've not known you for very long, you've helped me through a life-time of problems. Wherever we find ourselves in ten years, know that you saved me.

To Lizzy for sitting by me in the hospital when we thought I would never see my Mum again. There are no words for what that meant to me. And finally, to God, whilst I'm still not sure what or where you are, you helped my Mum beat cancer this year and without you there would certainly be no book. Thank you.

1 Introduction

Do you want a hot pot? asked Betty.

Ooh, that'd be lovely, Betty. Thank you, replied Deirdre. *I wonder if Peter will want some.*

Ooh, I wonder? responded Betty.

How Coronation Street is prime-time television, I will never know. It was another evening spent staring at the screen with my Nanna, watching the drudgery that is life in the Rovers Return, when my Nanna asked me: *What do you want to do when you're older?*

In a desperate attempt to cling on to the little life that I could feel ebbing away to the dulcet tones of Deirdre Barlow, I responded with enthusiasm:

> *Well, Nanna. I just want to help people. Fight for good, you know? Make this world a fairer and happier place. There is so much injustice in this world and I want to make a difference. I believe that all men and women are born equal and should be treated as such. I believe in equality of opportunity. I believe that under no circumstances should money take precedence over human rights. We should value others not because we can gain from them, but because they too are human. Our value comes not in doing, achieving or creating, but simply in being. As Ruskin states, 'There is no wealth but life', and I want to help people lead the best life they possibly can.*

Without a hint of sarcasm my Nanna replied, *And how much does that pay?*

I suppose that'll teach me to be less pretentious.

THE CURRENT STATE OF SOCIAL WORK

There is a dark cloud hanging over social work at the moment. I worry for those who have just started their journey into the field, or those who are considering it as a career, because much of the conversation around this profession is very off-putting. If you relied solely on mainstream media for information you would believe that social workers spend most of their time failing to protect children at risk while simultaneously putting happy and healthy children into care. Mind you, if you relied on mainstream media for all your information, I suspect negligent social workers may be the least of your problems, what with the imminent threat of world annihilation from swine flu, SARS and terrorism. The social work I see on the front pages is not the social work I know.

Social work is about so much more than Child Protection. Social workers specialise in mental health, disabilities, older people's care, sexual exploitation, domestic violence, fostering, adoption, homelessness, gangs and youth offending, to name but a few areas. We are a wide and varied bunch. And contrary to popular belief, social work *is* a good thing. Some people may find that statement uncomfortable, or even debatable but, at its core, social work is about making things better for people. And I believe that is a good thing. Of course, the process of helping people can become convoluted, warped and occasionally broken, but it is our job to ensure that doesn't happen.

We live in a time where being optimistic about change is made almost impossible. The economic situation is having a dramatic effect not only on the public sector but on the majority of British people. Increasing levels of poverty are creating more and more social problems. Again, if you relied on mainstream media, you'd be sure that it was people on benefits who caused the recession. We are living in desperate times. And while the Government points the finger of blame at everyone who has ever used the Welfare State, social workers are left to fix the ever-increasing number of problems. But of course social problems have been re-branded as individual problems, and social work is being forced to focus more on working with individuals than on looking at communities and the wider picture, thus making the task of creating social change an even harder one. We are literally expected to solve problems such as homelessness and youth crime one person at a time.

Have I sold social work to you yet?

Social work is complex and the more I know, the more I realise the depths of those complexities. I knew when I chose to be a social worker that there were things that would need improving. I liked the idea of being part of those changes. And while there has been, of late, a dark cloud hanging over us, I can see the sun beginning to break through. I believe it is a very exciting time to be a social worker as the discourse is always around change and improvement. There is a clear sense of always needing to better ourselves and put our arrogance aside in the name of good practice. There is definitely an air of hope around.

THE AIM OF THIS BOOK

This book has a very simple aim. I want to show you my journey into the profession and what social work has been like for me. I'm not trying to sell the profession to anyone. In fact, I think it takes a unique sort of person to want to do (and be good at) social work. Nor am I trying to put anyone off the profession. This book is simply my honest reflections of my experience (although the names and ages of people I work with have been changed for confidentiality reasons). So, if you are thinking about becoming a social worker; if you have just started the course; if you are newly qualified; or even if you have been in the profession for 20 years and are losing your passion for it, I hope that this book will help you have a clearer picture (or a reminder) of what social work is really like for those just starting out, and why some people still choose to do it.

What this book won't be is a guide to the best theory or practice examples. There are hundreds of people out there who can do that a lot better than me. Nor will it show you how I have integrated the Professional Capabilities Framework into my practice. If you are a student social worker you can figure it out for yourself, and if you're not a social worker at all, you won't thank me for introducing you to our assessment system. I wanted to strip away the jargon and focus on the emotional and human impact of the profession. I have included excerpts from my online blog, which was written at the time I was studying, to give you a sense of how I was really feeling at the time. On reviewing my blog, I realised that I relate most of my life experiences to some aspect of *The Lord of The Rings*. I'm not sure what that says about me but I have tried to keep my Frodo and Gollum references to a minimum in this book. Also, a few lovely and inspiring social workers I have met along the way have added their contributions about how the journey has been for them.

THE STRUCTURE OF THIS BOOK

This most sensible way to structure this book was chronologically. It begins with me choosing which course to take, progresses through two years of university, and ends with me qualifying. As a result, the reader will get a clear sense of what a roller-coaster of a journey I have been on and the rainbow of emotions I have experienced. I apologise in advance to you, the reader, if I give you a false sense of security that everything is positive, and then on the next page drag you into a pit of despair. I originally thought about warning you in advance if a depressing bit was coming up; but then I thought, sod it, life doesn't work like that. You don't get warned about the crisis phone calls you receive telling you one of your service users has been arrested, so if I have to go on the roller-coaster, you do too.

I'm sure you will have heard social work being described as a 'thankless task'; a description which could not be further from the truth. Yes, it is exhausting and repetitive and frustrating, and sometimes you feel like you are making no progress. But, once you sit back and reflect on what would happen if you were not there to offer the support you did, you begin to realise just how fantastic this job is. Even allowing someone to off load their anger or hurt for an hour is a great reward, knowing that they felt able to tell you about their problems. Simply having people know that you're there if they need you to be is a great feeling and an honour. And, very occasionally, you may end up saving someone's life.

Discovering you can get paid to help people

DECIDING AT SIXTEEN WHAT I WAS GOING TO DO FOR THE REST OF MY LIFE

I am very lucky, in the sense that I am one of those annoying people who knew from an early age what it was I was meant to do in life. I knew at five years old that I was going to be president of the United States of America. I was quite sure of it. Either that or a police officer. Unfortunately, my dream was shattered at the age of 11 when an insufferable know-it-all at school told me that you had to be American to be the president of America. I was devastated. I spent several years in a Bukowksi-esque state of turmoil, trying to decide who I was and what I was meant to be. Then someone from Barnardos gave a talk at our school about neglected and abused children and something clicked for me. From that point on I knew that I wanted a job which helped young, vulnerable children in need. I had no idea, however, that I wanted to be a social worker.

At age 16 a careers adviser came to school and informed us all that we needed to start deciding what job we wanted to progress towards. At that age we were convinced that we were essentially making a decision about what we would be doing for eternity, and so I knew I had to think this through carefully. I had never heard of social work; it was never mentioned at school and I was never aware of any classmates having or needing the help of a social worker. The only way I could think of helping people was through charity work. I researched the career paths charity workers had taken and the overwhelming majority seemed to have done a humanities degree at university. This suited me perfectly as history lessons were the main thing getting me to school at 16. I chose my A-levels (history, English literature, general studies and religious studies), managed to pass them, and applied for university to study history and politics.

Like most freshers, my first year at the University of Sheffield was a blur. I remember there being lectures, but mainly I remember behaving as if sleep, food and my liver were not important. While my freshers' year was amazingly fun, I had an overwhelming sense of guilt when July came round and I had failed all of my exams and spent all of my money. There are few talks in life which will re-motivate you more than explaining to your parents that for the whole of the past year, when you said you were 'working', you actually meant 'going to a party'. Luckily for me, my parents signed up for the whole 'unconditional love' thing.

I spent the summer of 2008 re-sitting nine exams and trying to give my life some sort of purpose again. I began researching online for volunteering opportunities which would enable me to work with vulnerable people. I was so desperate to restore my parents' faith in me that I applied for absolutely anything and everything. The first place to respond to my desperate emails was a Youth Justice Service. I had no experience of working with offenders and, in all honesty, I was nervous at the prospect of it.

MY FIRST EXPERIENCE OF VULNERABLE AND DANGEROUS CHILDREN

One of my first roles with the Youth Justice Service was as a support volunteer for a Summer Arts Programme. The aim was to help ten young boys, all on intensive criminal orders, achieve an arts award over a six-week period. Before I met the boys a planning meeting was held, and I learned about the seriousness of some of their crimes and the risks involved. Details were reeled off about thefts, burglaries, stabbings and drug dealing. At 19 years old I thought I knew a lot about the world and the city where I lived, but in that meeting I realised just how much I still had to learn.

On the first day, I walked into the classroom and my mind was screaming *CRIMINALS! THEY'RE ALL CRIMINALS. GET OUT, YOU IDIOT*. But before the voices in my head were able to convince me to leave, one of the boys came over and asked me who I was. Mikey was 17 years old and had a smile that stretched from one ear to the other. He was dressed in a bright green tracksuit and wore a cap so far down the back of his head that it made me doubt the laws of gravity. Within seconds of meeting me Mikey was passionately telling me about his love for Beyoncé: *It's not just that she's fit, she's also got a really good voice, you know*. Before I knew it, I was having a normal conversation with a funny and lovely young boy.

The first activity we took the boys on was a visit to a sculpture park to see a famous art exhibition. As soon as we arrived the curator of the park made a rather large point of telling the boys that they must not touch any of the exhibits. Within approximately 30 seconds of receiving this information I turned around to find 16-year-old Matthew, in tracksuit bottoms, balanced on top of a 20ft high stone rabbit. Initially, I was so in awe of his ability to climb such heights at such speed that it took me a few moments to realise that it was my job to get him down. I was reminded soon enough by the curator, who did not find Matthew's climbing skills as impressive as I did.

When we finally coaxed Matthew down, he was asked to wait in the car with me until the others had finished viewing the park. I was not expecting much conversation from someone with an inability to follow basic instructions, but again, I was very wrong.

After staring at a road sign for a few moments, Matthew asked me, *Is that where Margaret Thatcher closed the mines?*

Erm, I'm not sure, to be honest, I replied, clearly showing off all that I had learned from my politics degree so far.

Matthew then proceeded to tell me all about Thatcher's arguments with the miners and how he had read about it when he was in prison. Matthew also told me that he couldn't read before he went to prison, aged 14, and that being able to now was his proudest achievement.

After that first week my head was reeling with what an exciting, complex and fascinating group of young people I was working with. There was Paul, who had such a freakish ability to navigate his way round places he had never been to before that he nick-named himself 'Chav-Nav'. And 6ft 4in Carlton, who had committed a horrifically violent offence and yet was always the first to defend someone if he noticed they were being bullied.

I could not marry the boys' crimes with their personalities. Crime could not simply be a case of bad people doing bad things. As I began to learn more about the boys' upbringings, their stories gave me the facts I needed to back the feelings that I had been having for a long time; that crime has sociological reasons behind it. While they were all responsible for the crimes they committed, each one of them had experienced heartbreaking abuse or neglect as a child. It was part of my role to pick the boys up from home in the morning and drop them back at the end of the day. I remember picking Matthew up to find his Dad blind drunk by 8am, demanding Matthew return with food or money or not return at all. Of course these boys needed to learn that what they had done was wrong, but more than anything they needed the love and attention that all children deserve and they'd been denied. I was addicted from day one.

Saying that I was 'addicted from day one', is the best way I can think of to explain the feelings I was having. As most people who have ever worked with teenagers will know, the young person you are working with may look the same from day to day, but their personalities can change on an almost hourly basis; their dreams, goals, friends and plans change almost as frequently. Teenagers have the marmite effect on professionals. You either find their unpredictability incredibly exciting, or so frustrating that you want to cry.

The teenagers I was working with were like individual riddles. I wanted to know more about what caused them to commit crime; why they continued to commit crime despite not wanting to go to prison; why education wasn't working for them and what could be done to help them. I spent hours reading as much as I could about Youth Justice and based both my dissertations on youth crime. I continued to apply for volunteering roles to learn more about young people who offend and try to do something to help them. I volunteered in police stations, as a mentor in secure children's homes, and as an education support officer. I met hundreds of young people and returned home happy every day, knowing that I had found my calling. A flame was lit inside me, and when I have a bad day as a qualified social worker I remind myself of that feeling I had when I started.

THERE'S MORE TO HELPING PEOPLE
THAN MEANING WELL

Firm in the knowledge that I wanted to help young people all day, every day, I asked the woman who initially employed me as a Youth Justice volunteer what else I needed to do in order to make this happen. She told me that if I wanted to work with young people, it was worth doing a social work degree. I had heard of social work by now but, in all honesty, knew next to nothing about it. I certainly didn't think of social work as a 'profession'. I didn't give social work much more thought at all until a rather controversial arts and crafts session with a seven-year-old boy, who I was supporting, made me realise that I might be out of my depth.

I was being paid to give educational support to children who had parents with learning difficulties. One rainy Sunday afternoon, I told seven-year-old Nicholas that we would be having an art lesson and he could create whatever he wanted.

Nicholas asked with excitement, *Can we make towers?!*

Of course, I replied, cheerfully.

So, for an hour I helped Nicholas construct two large towers out of old boxes. After they were built, Nicholas surveyed his creation with displeasure.

Hmmm, he pondered, ominously.

Nicholas then ran upstairs and brought down a box of paper planes he had made at school and began placing them, one by one, in the windows of the towers.

It's the American towers! he pointed out, helpfully.

My heart stopped. I had unwittingly assisted Nicholas in creating a sculpture of the 9/11 atrocity. Knowing my luck, I thought, either MI6 will probably catch wind of this and have me arrested, or it would be all over the front page of *The Daily Mail* by the morning: *SOCIAL CARE WORKER ENCOURAGES TERRORISM*.

I knew the professional reaction was not to scream and fall to my knees, but that was the extent of my knowledge. There must be a way of handling this without making Nicholas feel like he had created an awful piece of art and shattering his self-esteem, I thought. But what if he knew that this was wrong and offensive, I argued with myself. Should I be calling Mental Health Services? Or the police? Finally, I concluded, I needed to get better at this job.

That evening I decided to find out more about social work. I searched on the internet and before I knew it four hours had passed. It was as if I had found a box of treasure buried in some sand. I became so mesmerised with what seemed to be 'the perfect job' that I spent hours and hours reading as much as I could about how to become a social worker.

I couldn't believe that people could get trained with specialist skills and knowledge to 'support people who have been socially excluded' as well as 'advocate for vulnerable people'. Sentences such as *social workers fight for social justice and human rights* made me wonder where had this job had been all my life.

That evening I ran back to my student house and burst into the living room.

Have you seen this? I declared, holding up mass amounts of print-outs about social work. *You can actually GET PAID TO HELP PEOPLE! Can you believe that? I can get PAID to do the stuff I do now for FREE!*

Only one of my nine flatmates looked up from the television screen to acknowledge my enthusiasm. *That's nice*, he said. Their lack of enthusiasm didn't matter; I was in love.

PROVING TO THE CAREERS ADVISER THAT, ACTUALLY, I WAS NOT TOO YOUNG TO DO SOCIAL WORK

The careers adviser at university had told me not to bother applying for a Masters in social work because, at age 21, I would not be old enough to be accepted on the course due to lack of experience. I did not think it would be wise to admit to her that I had spent the majority of my time at university volunteering, rather than studying, so went away quietly convinced that she was wrong.

I had just about the right grades and the right experience to apply to do a Masters course and so for the next few months I set about applying for places and attending interviews. I was desperate to get on the course. I was convinced that this was the job I was meant to do and that I had found my calling. For months I tried to memorise everything Neil Thompson and Adams, Dominelli and Payne had ever written. I had set answers for all the difficult questions: *Anti-oppressive practice is...*, *Social justice is...*, *social work gets a bad press because...* I was ready, and I knew I was. I was confident about my skills, confident about my basic knowledge, and confident that I wanted to do this job. In hindsight, if I had not felt this way then it would not have been right to apply, because over the next few years my confidence would be shattered and re-built several hundred times over.

The journey I was about to embark on was more challenging than anything I could have imagined. There are many jobs similar to social work. It shares aspects of teaching, nursing, policing, psychology and law, and yet, at the same time, social work is unique. Unless you have worked in social services in a support role for several years, nothing can fully prepare you for the reality of social work. My wide and varied range of experience was the best preparation I could have had. The idealism, optimism and passion I had for helping people at the start of my social work journey would make some of the disappointing realities of social work very hard to take, but I shall come to this later.

I was accepted on to the Masters Course in three different cities, but choosing Sheffield was a no-brainer. I would like to say that I chose it because it had the best reputation out of the three courses, which it did, but it was mainly because I was so happy with the friends (and bars) I'd met in Sheffield that leaving was not an option.

Starting the course and meeting Spider-Man

STARTING THE COURSE

By the time I arrived at my first lecture I could confidently reel off a spiel of memorised text from one of the core social work textbooks on the recommended reading list. I knew how to say what social workers do, but when I think back it is quite amazing how little I really knew about the role.

If I am being totally honest, I thought the social work course would be pretty easy. After three years of filtering through piles of the densest research on political statistical analysis, I was sure that learning about people's problems would be a holiday. To my shame and disadvantage, I did not think of social work as a profession. When I thought of professionals I thought of doctors, lawyers and teachers. I did not think that social workers would require the same expertise.

I have never been happier to be so wrong.

As the course agenda was handed round, I noticed that the list of topics and assignments for term one was unnervingly long. We were set several pieces of work before we were let into the big, wide world, to prove that we were ready to work with real people with real problems. This was called our 'Readiness to Practice Portfolio' and it had to be completed over the first four months. As I stared at the course agenda I had a slow and horrible realisation that in order to pass the first term alone, I would have to spend the next 100 days writing three essays, undergoing two practical assignments as well as learning the law, policy, skills, knowledge and values for working within Children's Services, Mental Health Services and Older Person's Services. I had started the course hoping to learn a bit more about Youth Justice but was faced with this barrage of work. Political Statistical Analysis had a new contender for the 'course with the most ridiculous amount of work' award.

I am sure that those who have studied law or medicine will be scoffing at my indignation over the course agenda. In fact, I remember moaning to an old friend who had begun studying law at the same time I started my Masters. Her response was a rather unsympathetic, *Yeah, well I have six exams in three days, so take your problems elsewhere.* But like I said, when I started I did not have a full understanding of the professional aspect of the job, and part of me genuinely thought that social work would be a purely practical course.

MY SHADOWING NIGHTMARE

Professors encourage you to keep an open mind with regard to what you may wish to specialise in. While I had enrolled on the course to become a Youth Justice practitioner, I decided that I would indeed keep my options open, just in case I discovered something that might ignite my passion even further. That said, however, I was very confident that I did not want to work in mental health. I was always quite astonished, when introducing myself to people on my course, to find that people were hoping to have a career in Mental Health Services. I recognised that it was an essential service, and a worthy job to have, but to actively want to work in that area was, and still is, a foreign concept to me, for very personal reasons.

One of the 'Readiness to Practice' practical assignments was to shadow a social worker for the day. We had no say over who we would shadow, or which area of practice we would be going into. We simply had to wait for a call from a social worker and arrange a day. The call came … and it was my worst nightmare.

Hello, is that Rebecca? said the cheery voice.

Yes, it is, I replied excitedly.

Hi, my name's Liz, I'm a social worker in a mental health team…

The rest, I don't remember. All I can recall is the room closing in on me and my whole body becoming uncomfortably hot. I know I sound dramatic, but, at that point, I was genuinely scared of the prospect of working in mental health.

I was halfway through desperately trying to word an email to my tutor (that did not make explicit how pathetic I was being, but that would allow me to get out of the assignment), when I experienced a strong pang of guilt. I was ashamed of my aversion and my fear of mental health. As I read the excuses I had hurriedly written, the better angels in my head shouted at me *what is the worst that could happen?* And so I consigned myself to a day in Mental Health Services.

Little did those angels know that, within two hours of starting the shadowing, someone would try to stab me. But never mind; they meant well.

MY DAY IN THE PSYCHIATRIC WARD

Liz was a lovely social worker. She was organised, efficient, on time, clever and, most of all, genuinely concerned about the people she worked with. She liked her service users and they liked her. She remembered the little things that mattered to them and she took the time to listen to their concerns. It was a pleasure shadowing Liz.

The first place she took me to was a low-security psychiatric ward. I think the term for this is 'baptism of fire'. Like most people, my knowledge of psychiatric wards was shaped by

Hollywood films and this quiet and hidden-away psychiatric ward in the depths of North Yorkshire did not disappoint. It was something straight out of a Stanley Kubrick movie. The building felt like an uneasy cross between a Victorian public swimming bath and a modern-day hospital. There was so much white; the floors were white, the walls were white, the beds were white, the gowns were white. It was sterile and saddening.

As I walked down a long, brightly lit corridor, a frail old Indian man shuffled towards me in the opposite direction. He was being escorted at snail's pace by what seemed to be an unnecessarily large male nurse. As we got closer, I could see he was smiling at me and raising his hand. He had such a sweet and welcoming smile, so naturally I smiled back. He began to lift his hand when suddenly the male guard/nurse firmly grabbed his wrist and calmly said *No, don't stab the nice lady with the pencil.* The old man looked very disappointed at this directive.

I stopped in astonishment. Why had he wanted to stab me? He seemed so friendly. Liz laughed and hurried me along.

Now, of course, the majority of psychiatric wards are not like this one. Nor are the patients likely to have a vendetta against you the moment you step through the door. I can already hear Mental Health social workers screaming at me for perpetuating the negative Hollywood stereotypes. I have been to numerous wards since, and worked with very unwell young people, and never had an experience like that again. That morning I was just unlucky.

Nonetheless, it was not the start I was hoping for. My unease about the day increased.

Liz had taken me to the psychiatric ward first to show me what can happen if all other interventions fail and why it is so important to identify and address issues early. It was a valuable lesson which I have not forgotten. The next place she took me was a care home for older people with dementia.

DAVID DICKINSON IS NOT TO BE TRUSTED

The home was in a beautiful location. Ivy climbed the tall walls of the red-bricked house. On arrival the reception staff were jovial and there was a lively atmosphere. We had come to see Elsie, who was waiting in the common room.

The common room was a large, carpeted living room with 30 large, comfy chairs lining three walls. The fourth wall was dominated by a large television and a bookshelf filled solely with hundreds of Jilly Cooper books. I hope that if I ever have to be placed in an old people's home they will ask me what books I want to read. Not that I have anything against Jilly Cooper of course, it's just that there's only so much adultery and show-jumping a person can take.

Most of the 30 chairs around the room were occupied by residents. Some of them were chatting, others were doing word searches; and then there was Elsie. Elsie was sitting in a big, red leather chair which only served to highlight how incredibly tiny she was. Her feet were not even attempting to touch the floor and her elbows could only *just* perch themselves on the sides of the chair. The majority of her was covered by a thick lilac blanket, except her head which had a large mass of silver hair mounded upon it like a smooth pineapple. She had a very beautiful face and an even better personality.

Elsie was very alert. She could recollect details well and, while she didn't like to talk much, when she did, she was very kind. Liz asked her about how she was liking the home and whether she wanted anything to be changed. Elsie seemed happy. When we left I had to ask Liz why Elsie was in the home. It seemed a waste for her to be there if she could manage at home. That's when Liz informed me that Elsie was thoroughly convinced that David Dickinson was stealing her antiques.

For those of you who don't know, David Dickinson is that man from *Bargain Hunt* who is one suntan away from cremation. Elsie was convinced that every time *Bargain Hunt* came on the television, David began flogging her antiques. To be honest, I've never trusted the man and I wouldn't put it past him. However, Elsie was so sure of this fact that she began securing her belongings and refused to leave the house.

While it seemed unfair that Elsie could be so able in most aspects of her life and yet have one aspect ruin it, I was impressed by the care she was receiving in the care home. It did not feel like a home where people go to wait out the end of their days, which is how I often hear it described, but rather it was filled with fascinating people who had the full attention of well trained staff. It was a perfect model of the standard we should expect from all facilities like this.

My final visit was to Bernard, a 70-year-old man living in his own home. Bernard had been diagnosed with Parkinson's Disease Dementia a few months previous. Bernard was an inspiration. In his youth he had travelled the world. He'd lived in India, Australia and Paris. He'd fallen in love with the girl of his dreams, married her and lived happily ever after until her death ten years earlier. While he had never had children, he had worked as a professor of philosophy and his intelligence shone through. Everything he said was worth saying and worth hearing.

Bernard was at a heart-breaking stage of life where he had all his faculties, and was astute and alert enough to be fully aware that all of that was going to fade away as the years progressed. For me, the cruellest aspect of dementia is when you are aware that you are ill and aware that it will get worse. I find some peace in those dementia sufferers who are so badly affected that they don't know that they are not experiencing reality. Watching Bernard and listening to everything he had done and everything he knew, I felt as if I was talking to a dying man. Even though his physical health could remain excellent for the next 30 years, his mental ability would be gone long before then.

Liz's job was to make sure that the support would already be in place for Bernard when things started to get really bad. As Bernard was a widower he had selected two younger friends to be his carers. Bernard received a personalised budget and was using that to pay his friends to check on him twice a day, do his shopping and other basic tasks. It was a great comfort to Bernard to have people he knew caring for him, rather than a stranger. Pride is a common feature among people I have met from the war generation. Bernard wanted his carers to know him as the fiercely intelligent and independent man he was, and to act accordingly and appropriately when his capability decreased.

It was comforting to know that Bernard was able to avoid a care home, which, in his own words, he described as being completely *unsuitable for someone as intolerant of others as me*. He was visibly content with the support he was receiving from Liz. He had few queries for her and instead spent half an hour showing a genuine interest in me and my social work journey. Liz and Bernard clearly had a great professional relationship, and as we vacated Bernard's house I was left with an incredibly positive feeling. My day may have had a rocky start, but it had a great finish.

IDENTIFYING YOUR LIMITS

My day in Mental Health Services was definitely a memorable one. It taught me a lot of lessons about the importance of early intervention to prevent crises and to prevent people from being placed in residential care settings. It also showed me the value of personalisation. Liz knew each one of her service users as an individual and treated them as such. As a result they felt listened to and important.

I learned just how little I knew about mental health, particularly dementia. Until I met Liz, Bernard and Elsie, I had no idea that dementia was an umbrella term for a wide range of diseases which affect the brain. I realised how little I knew about the law concerning mental health, and how important it is to ensure that people's legal rights are maintained when they become incapable of defending themselves. Overall, I learned that mental health is nothing to be scared of. My previous associations with mental health were of depressing, chaotic lives with unhappy endings. My day with Liz had shown me that does not have to be the case.

Did it make me want to be a mental health social worker? No. But it has made me a better children's social worker. Mental ill-health is unavoidable in social work, regardless of your specialism. I dread to think what an awful practitioner I would be today if I still held the negative perception that I had started with. By pushing myself to the limits I was able to firmly identify what my limits were. Identifying your limits is, as I would continue to learn, a key skill to becoming a successful social worker.

The second of our practical assignments was, thankfully, a lot less dramatic, although I did get to meet Spider-Man.

PICKING MY TARGET

The first essay the university set us was a piece on child development. After three or four lectures on the works of Piaget, Vygotsky, Bowlby, Ainsworth and Erikson, we were given the task of shadowing a pre-school child for half a day to learn about observation and assessment of children's development. We were randomly assigned nurseries and so one

Monday afternoon I found myself standing in a room full of tiny people deciding which one to follow. (I would like to point out at this stage that the children's parents had given consent for me to follow their children!)

The nursery I had been assigned was located at the base of a large, run-down tower block. When I was first given the address I was certain there had been a mistake. The tower block was renowned for hosting illegal raves. I couldn't envisage how there could be a nursery in the same building. But there it was, sitting unassumingly at the bottom of the flats.

The children who attended the nursery were from some of the poorest families in the city. Fully aware of this fact, the nursery ensured that there was no uniform code (to save on parental expenses), and free breakfast, lunch, snacks and dinner were provided. I noticed almost immediately that the walls were very bare. My memories of nursery were of colourful collages on every surface; it was chaotic and inspiring. When I asked the head teacher why this nursery's walls were so blank, she gave me a fascinating insight into how and why the nursery functioned as it did.

The walls were kept blank in an attempt to maintain a sense of calm. The effect of poverty meant that there were high rates of abuse, neglect, drug misuse and criminal behaviour among the children's families. Within their home life lay chaos, and therefore nursery had to become their stable base.

Additionally, the children's homes were filled with risk and danger. To my utter shock there was a play box full of sharp nails, hammers and wood. As we were in a room of children aged between three and five years old I was sure that this box must have been carelessly left by builders. The head teacher again informed me that the box was there to teach the children how to behave around dangerous things. They learned to avoid the box entirely or, if they were interested in it, they learned how to handle things with care, avoiding the 'pointy end'. While the notion of it still upsets me, I could see how this was a particularly valuable lesson for children who often might be left among discarded needles at home.

MEETING SPIDER-MAN

I selected a blond four-year-old boy named William to follow. He seemed fairly quiet and was not really associating with the other children much. We had been given strict instructions not to interact with our subjects in order to be able to record their natural behaviour. For the first 30 minutes I sat across the room from William, watching him from a distance.

The children had been given an hour of unstructured play. William had a habit of selecting a task on his own, and the moment another person came to join him he would move on to another task on his own. I immediately found myself worried about this child. Is he okay? Does he have friends? Is he getting bullied? My concerns for William resulted in me completely ignoring the one instruction we had been given from our tutors and going nearer to where he was.

You okay? I asked.

Mhmm, he replied without looking up from his painting.

I sat down a metre away from him and watched as he painted with intensity what can only be described as a butterfly from a psychological blot test.

Wow! I said. *That's brilliant. I would put that up on my wall if I were you.*

William looked at me and frowned. *I've offended him*, I thought, *and I have no idea why. Understanding children is impossible.* As I was thinking this, William had found a large sheet of paper in the cupboard next to him and placed it over the painting. He began rubbing his hands all over the painting, as if to smudge it. When he had finished he peeled the two sheets of paper apart and handed me the top copy.

For you. One for me, one for you, he said.

William had effectively photocopied the painting for me. I was touched. But no nearer to understanding the child.

He packed away his paints and another young girl came over. She asked how he had made two copies of the painting. Expecting William to walk away from the inquisitive young girl, I was shocked when he patiently took her through the process again with her own painting. Once she had got the hang of it he walked off on his own again. William clearly had social skills. *Ohhh, I see. He's a maverick*, I reassuringly told myself.

For the rest of the session I left William alone. I initially hadn't been aware of him carrying a notepad which, every so often, he would take from his pocket and write a few sentences in. However, he hadn't learned the alphabet yet, so the letters all looked like variations of the number two. It was fascinating watching him stop himself mid-walk to take note of something he had seen outside, or after he had talked to a nursery assistant. He would only write for a few seconds and then put the pad away again. I restrained myself from inquiring as to why he did this until the end of the day. At 4pm I packed my things away and approached him.

William.

Mhmm, he replied, still largely uninterested in me.

What have you been writing in your notepad?

Information of interest, he responded, while sorting his crayons in size order. I paused, not knowing how to inquire further. Luckily, William cleared up my confusion by stating, *I'm Peter Parker.*

As in Spider-Man? I responded. William obviously thought this question was stupid, as, rather than answer me, he simply pulled out his arm from his jumper to reveal a Spider-Man transfer tattoo which was peeling off after several baths.

But you can't tell anyone, he warned me, making eye contact with me for the first time that day.

I promised him I wouldn't and left.

On the walk home I couldn't stop thinking about how interesting William had been to watch. I don't know whether it was the fact that it was a hot day, or the fact that I had skipped lunch, but I found myself wondering what would happen if William really was a young Spider-Man and everyone ignored him because he was a child. Needless to say, I didn't get a fantastic mark on my final essay with my thoughts centring around whether or not William really was a superhero.

READY TO PRACTISE

The first term passed without any glitches, although I scraped through the law exam. I have always struggled to revise, and having to memorise the legal framework for adult social care was almost the death of me. The Children Acts and Mental Health Acts made much more sense. There was structure to them. Adult social care was made up of what felt like 1,000 Parliamentary Acts, and I have no shame in saying I struggled to retain all that information ready to get it down on paper during one particular hour on a Tuesday morning. Exams are horrific.

Approximately five days before completing my Masters, it was announced that changes would be made to adult legislation to combine the 32 different pieces of it into one. While this is obviously a great thing, I do remember screaming at the computer with bitterness when I read it. Better late than never, I suppose.

After proving I had the basic knowledge, skills and values necessary to practise as a social worker, I waited nervously for word of my first 100-day placement.

4 Single-handedly saving the world

AUNT PAT

Before I applied to be a social worker, I read a brilliant and moving book by Shy Keenan. It begins: *I was born and broken in Birkenhead. I was unwanted, beaten, sold, swapped, photographed, filmed, left for dead, corrupted, blamed, betrayed and ignored.* The next 300 pages detail Shy's story of growing up, the abuse she experienced, how it affected her and how she made it to adulthood. It is a tough read; hard enough to see on paper, never mind experience first-hand. There is a paragraph towards the end, however, which is so simple and so powerful that after reading it I copied it out, word-for-word, in my neatest writing, and pinned it on the wall next to my bed. Every time I woke up I saw these words:

> *Many people ask me how I was able to survive my childhood and my answer is always the same – good people like my Aunt Pat and Uncle Ken and my Nanny and Grandpa Wallbridge. Their tiny ray of light in my dark miserable childhood gave me hope, balance and a dream of better to cling onto. It was a classic case of good over bad and despite the fact that there was a great deal of bad, it amazes me even to this day, that the little bit of good I found back then, was enough to save me, but it was and it did. So, if I'm ever asked how we can help children we don't know are victims, I would always say, do your best to be someone's Aunt Pat or Uncle Ken.*
> —Shy Keenan, *Broken*, Hodder Paperbacks, p 229

These words, for me, captured the simplicity and value of what it is to help someone. I wanted to be an Aunt Pat.

THE PERFECT PLACEMENT AND THE WORST VOICE MAIL

A month before placement was due to start I received an email from my tutor, informing me that I had received a placement offer but that they had been having difficulty contacting me. The placement was with a local housing trust which I had learned a lot about during my time volunteering with the Youth Justice Service. The trust worked with young offenders and other teenagers who were in need of independent accommodation. It was perfect, and I desperately wanted to do it.

I hurriedly contacted the trust on the phone, only to be met by an answering machine. Due to my over excitement at the prospect of working there, the voicemail I left was not one of my finest messages. When I hung up, I realised that I hadn't mentioned my name or finished the message with a proper sentence; but rather had ended with something along the lines of: *hearing from you will be… I look forward to… thank you.*

Panicking, I rang straight back to explain myself. This time the manager answered. She had a broad Yorkshire accent. *Hi, this is Rebecca Novell. I'm ringing to apologise for the voicemail I just left…* Without a doubt my favourite quality of my first placement manager, Poppy, would end up being her unashamed honesty. *You sounded like a right idiot,* were the first words she said to me, *It gave me a right good laugh to listen to though.* My cheeks swelled red with embarrassment. Poppy told me to come in the next day for an informal interview *to make sure* I could *speak in sentences.*

ROUGH AREA

The trust was situated in a notorious area of the city, one well-known for sexual exploitation, gang exploitation, high levels of crime and even higher levels of poverty. It is common knowledge that you don't go to this area after nightfall. I'd be lying if I didn't say I was nervous about working there. I tentatively got on the bus to meet Poppy and successfully convinced her to accept me as her student. A few weeks later my first placement began.

Those who lived in the area were predominantly of African descent and as a result the local shops and restaurants were completely foreign to me. For the first month I felt completely out of my depth with regard to eating out for lunch; I never recognised anything on any of the menus. Fortunately, my Somali colleague took me under his wing and showed me what to order. The food was, without a doubt, one of the highlights of that placement, and as a result I've developed an unhealthy addiction to Harissa.

The more I got to know the local shop owners the more I began to wonder where the area had got its bad reputation from. Admittedly, I only worked there during the day, but from what I could see it was one of the best areas in the city. Unlike anywhere else I had visited, this area had a palpable sense of community. Much of the socialising centred around the mosques and churches. It was apparent that everyone knew each other. If there was anything you needed you could guarantee that someone nearby would be able to help you. People were always outdoors on the street, young and old, eating and talking together. I began seeing how the care and consideration of neighbours could have a hugely positive impact on individuals. There was always a welcoming and inclusive atmosphere which made it almost impossible to ever feel lonely.

The community I was working in appeared to be a fairly inclusive and egalitarian group and prompted me to question what the '*social*' in '*social work*' stood for. I began wondering how much less people would rely on social services and the care of strangers if we simply all looked out for each other a bit more. This vibrant, chaotic and misunderstood neighbourhood sparked the beginning of my deep and ongoing concern with the profes-sionalisation of social work – which I shall come to later.

MY FIRST CASE LOAD

I was incredibly excited to have my own case load. I had plenty of experience working with people one-on-one, but to have to work with five or six young people and support a wide range of needs was a completely new challenge. Without sounding too big-headed, I took to the challenge with ease. I have always been an extremely organised person. My partner jokes that one of my favourite hobbies is making lists. It's not really a joke but more of an accurate observation. My Filofax always travels with me, and I can usually tell you what I will be doing at 4pm on a Monday in six months time.

My job was to assess young people, aged between 16 and 21, who were referred to our service. I would have to establish whether we could meet their needs and, if it was decided that we could, I would help them move into one of our shared or self-contained flats. Once a young person had moved in with us a lot of the work involved assisting with practical tasks such as showing them how to top up their gas and electric cards, or help-ing them register with a dentist. By meeting with the young person three times a week, we would decide upon some goals that they would work towards while they stayed with us. I got my first taste of professional multi-agency meetings with schools, the police and other social workers. It was straightforward but exciting nonetheless.

Meeting my new service users was motivating. I enjoyed knowing that I would have a major role in ensuring that each young person I was being introduced to would reach their desired goals. The paperwork was easy enough, and this being the voluntary sector there was not too much of it. Completing assessments and following support plans was relatively simple, or at least I thought so, initially. All the classic advice about time man-agement, preparation and good note-keeping proved to be valuable. Things were going well. There were, however, many lessons that I had yet to learn.

BE INQUISITIVE

One sunny Wednesday afternoon, a Somali boy called Ibrahim attended the office look-ing for housing. There was nothing particularly remarkable about him at first sight. Due to the very little English he spoke, and the fact that I spoke even less Somali, the likelihood of me being able to help him looked slim. Luckily, my colleague knew of a local man who had volunteered to translate for anyone who needed it. I called him, and within five min-utes he was at the office. The translator was able to ask Ibrahim if he was happy for him to translate on his behalf, and so the assessment began.

Ibrahim was 16 years old. He described how he had travelled to Greece from Somalia after his whole family had been murdered by what Ibrahim described as his Dad's busi-ness partners. Alone, he had made it to Europe. On arrival in Greece he had received no support and spent eight months sleeping on a bench in a park with other displaced refugees. Desperate for a more stable life, Ibrahim travelled in the back of a lorry until he somehow found himself in Yorkshire. It was time to see what England could do to help him. My conversation with him was difficult and eye-opening.

After the assessment, Ibrahim left the office and began heading towards a 40-year-old white man who was waiting outside in a silver Mercedes. I hurriedly asked the translator to call Ibrahim back. I asked Ibrahim who this man was. He informed me that the man had found him sleeping under a bridge one day and had let him come back to his house. The man had fed and clothed Ibrahim and was helping him to find accommodation. As a fresh-faced student, my first reaction was to think what a Good Samaritan this man was being. My manager, however, being as experienced as she was, sensed something wasn't quite right.

Do you have to do anything in return for him helping you? she inquired. Ibrahim informed us that the man had told him that once he was settled and had begun to receive some form of income, he would then have to pay him 50 per cent of everything he received. Ibrahim also mentioned how the man made him feel uncomfortable as he liked to touch him on the leg a lot.

I was horrified. My heart was in my mouth. If Poppy hadn't asked Ibrahim these questions, I would have simply let him get back into the car with this man. I thought I had asked everything I needed to know. The reality was that I had asked Ibrahim everything on the trust's assessment form and nothing more. That was the first time I realised that an assessment is only as good as the assessor. A form can never cater for all individuals in all situations. The key is to be inquisitive; nosey, even. Knowing what questions to ask that weren't provided for me would only come with learning and experience.

I learned a lot from Ibrahim. What particularly stuck with me was just how incomprehensible the experiences of asylum seekers are. The majority of them will be dealing with extreme loss, be it the death of a family member or all their family members as in Ibrahim's case, or the experience of your entire community being wiped out by war or famine. This trauma can lead to heightened anxiety and other mental health problems, and also decreases asylum seekers' ability to trust authority figures, such as the police and social workers.

The moment they arrive in the United Kingdom they are subjected to horrific racism and vilification from the national media, which provokes verbal and physical attacks from ill-educated members of the public. Once they have entered the UK they become immediately de-skilled. An individual who may have been a qualified doctor in their own country is now unemployed, unemployable and homeless. They are subject to humiliation as they have to beg for help just to stay alive because full financial support is not granted to those who have not successfully secured asylum. They are expected to navigate a foreign culture which demands that they know the legal, health and social security system. And, simultaneously, they anxiously await the decision which determines whether or not they will be returned to the hell from which they came.

Asylum seekers and refugees are some of the strongest, most incredible, most inspiring people I have ever had the honour to work with. To survive one of the multitude of traumas they have been faced with is a tremendous achievement; to survive them all and continue to thrive afterwards is nothing short of miraculous.

OFFICE POLITICS

Some of my cohort were very unhappy with their placements. I heard horror stories of someone having to spend seven hours of their day watching a service user packing boxes in a warehouse. A very empowering experience for the service user, I'm sure! While I adored my first placement, it certainly wasn't perfect.

Something you can never be prepared for unless you are a permanent part of a team is office politics. As a volunteer, staff usually make an effort to put on a professional face. When you become part of the staff you soon realise that work teams are like families; and like many families, some are highly dysfunctional.

I was working in a team of five people out of a total office of ten. We were a small team compared to other statutory settings. While it created a definite sense of camaraderie, as everyone knew everything about everyone else, it also meant that tensions could run high as you listened to the same people's problems every single day. I had never thought to factor in the impact that office politics could have on the ability of staff to provide a good service. I had always assumed that all adults would act as complete professionals in the work place. In reality, if team members actively dislike each other then the team can become highly dysfunctional and ineffective. While disputes in the trust I worked for did not detract from the job at hand, I have subsequently worked in teams where the focus on service users has been lost. I dread to think what sort of social worker I would have been if I had been trained in a team like that.

As a qualified social worker, I recently had a student shadow me who was in a dysfunctional and insular team. Everything she spoke about with regard to her placement was about the team and her colleagues; not once did she mention the problems or successes of her service user group. She was exhausting all her energy on trying to avoid being unpopular at work. I cannot stress enough to students who find themselves in this situation, that they report it to their university as soon as possible. While your university may not be able to wave a magic wand and make everything better, they will be able to offer advice on psychological and organisational theories which could provide you with some essential 'professional' survival skills. Office politics is the least worthy hurdle to stumble at when it comes to pursuing social work as a career.

NOTE TO SELF: DON'T FALL ASLEEP AT WORK

For five of the weeks I was on placement the trust employed Said, an agency staff member, to carry a small case load. I still cry with laughter when I think about some of the things Said did. Luckily, none of his behaviour crossed the border into dangerous practice, but he was certainly the inspiration for how not to practise social work.

My favourite example of Said's inspiring behaviour was during some joint-working we had to do after a fight had occurred in one of our properties. One of his service users had tried to strangle one of my mine. Both young people were safe, but the incident had been reported to the police and so we had to meet an officer at the property. We supported the officer in accessing our CCTV footage and proceeded to give statements. We sat in the officer's car, myself in the front and Said in the back. The officer took my statement first.

For those who have never had to do it, giving a police statement is an amazingly laborious and time-consuming activity. A five-minute statement can easily take 40 minutes to record. As I was 20 minutes into my statement I heard a faint rumbling noise coming from inside the car. The officer did not seem to notice it and so I continued, undeterred. But as the rumbling became louder, it began to bother me. I had never heard a car make that noise before. I started to look around while still concentrating on the task in hand. It was then, in my wing mirror, that I caught a glimpse of Said, head slumped to the back of his seat, mouth wide open, snoring like a baby elephant. The officer noticed what I was looking at and turned around to look at Said (and the small patch of dribble that had landed on his shirt) in disgust. She promptly woke Said up, but did not receive the apology she was clearly expecting. Said did not stay with the trust much longer after that.

Even the negative parts, however, were extremely useful in developing me as a social worker. From that day on I knew I never wanted to be the person who fell asleep in meetings. That was not the social worker I was going to be.

SUICIDE ATTEMPT

I bumbled through my first few weeks of placement trying desperately to make sure that the young people I had been allocated engaged with the service. I had also learned to call them 'service users' rather than 'kids' (a term my manager despised). Progress was steady and fulfilling, and none of my cases had been too out of the ordinary.

Then one very sunny Thursday afternoon, I made my usual home visit to Mick, a 19-year-old man suffering from severe anxiety. To this day, Mick is still one of the loveliest and most polite people I have ever met. Every other word he said was a *please* or a *thank you* and he was always so apologetic when he took up anyone's time. He was the embodiment of a gentle giant. At 6ft 5in tall, I remember always being amazed by the soft tone and low volume of Mick's voice. I was even more amazed when I found out that Mick was a champion boxer; this was the same person who apologised to car drivers for holding them up when he was crossing the road, even though they had stopped at the traffic lights. He was a sweet and gentle young man, and a pleasure to work with.

On this unremarkable Thursday afternoon I knocked on the door and waited for Mick to answer. No answer came. I knocked again. As you may have gathered, Mick was not one for letting people down. Slightly concerned, I let myself into Mick's flat with the master key and called for him. *Mick?* I shouted. Again, no answer came.

As I walked through the living room, I heard the sound of smashed glass coming from the kitchen. I quickly located my phone in case I had to make an emergency call. I approached the kitchen and saw Mick standing with his back to the door. He was staring out of the window.

It was then I noticed the knife in his hand. *Mick, it's Rebecca. Talk to me.* Mick replied quietly, *Hi Rebecca.*

Mick, are you okay? What are you holding that knife for? I said, with as calm a voice as possible.

I'm going to kill myself, Mick said in a matter-of-fact way. My hand hovered over the phone in my pocket.

For the next 20 minutes I calmly talked with Mick to establish what had led him to this point and, vitally, to get him to put the knife down. I would be lying if I said that I remember the conversation. The 20 minutes I was there felt like 30 seconds, and was a frantic mixture of yelling support from my manager, assessing the danger to Mick, and assessing the danger to myself. Eventually, however, Mick put the knife down and agreed to see someone from the mental health team, despite his fear of being sectioned. After the crisis was over it was time to go home.

That feeling I had when walking home was one I will remember for the rest of my life. The magnitude of what had happened was sinking in and there was a realisation that things might have ended very differently if I had not been there. It's difficult to describe the feeling I had without coming across as incredibly self-congratulatory and smug. In social work, however, it is these moments that you have to cling on to. You can go days without seeing much obvious progress and be left with a sense of futility. Then you get a 20 minute slot, maybe once every few months, where you are there to help stop someone from killing themselves. That one moment and that one person's life makes the rest of the frustration more than worthwhile. As I walked home I felt like I was floating. I smiled at everyone; there was so much colour to everything.

But with the immense highs came the inevitable lows.

EVA

ARE YOU STUPID? screamed the voice outside. *I KNOW MY RIGHTS. YOU CAN'T TREAT US LIKE THIS.* These are the first words I heard from Eva, and the start of a long and emotional journey which drastically redefined my view of social work. Eva was a petite young woman with hair that changed colour every week and a smile that lit up the room. My experience over the next ten months would lead me to write the following blog on my website:

Cup of tea and a chat

I want to tell you about a young girl that I recently worked with. For the purposes of confidentiality, I cannot tell you her name, her age or the context in which I was working with her. But I do want you to know about her.

Eva arrived at my office waiting for an assessment. Most young people who arrive at our office will sit quietly and nervously, unsure about the service we offer. Not Eva. She strode in shouting about her rights and entitlements. She knew what she was owed and she wanted it NOW. All the young people in reception took an immediate dislike to her. I thought she was brilliant.

From the background information I had on Eva, I knew she had effectively brought herself up from the age of six. She was the embodiment of resilience. Her parents were alive but had nothing to do with her. Occasionally, they drove past her in the street and would wave – but never stop. She had been severely let down by a social worker who, at the age of ten, placed her to live with a neglectful male who was no relation to the family but had occasionally done the gardening for Eva's Grandma. When that foster placement fell through, Eva drifted from friend's house to friend's house and by the time she arrived to me she was living at the home of a 40-year-old male who was well-known to the police for violent offences. Social services should have been involved and yet Eva was one of those children who managed to slip under the radar by not attending school and changing address frequently.

My first keywork session with Eva was explaining to her that the Sexual Exploitation Service had extreme concerns about her. Explaining to a young girl who has spent time living on the streets, lived with numerous non-familial males, and managed to feed and clothe herself for the last few years without much help, that some adults who do not know her think she may be 'vulnerable', is not a fun task I can assure you. For the first ten minutes I had the words WHO DO THEY THINK THEY ARE?! and I'M GONNA SMASH THEIR HEADS IN shouted at me. But once that was over we had a good and honest conversation about how her life looks to other people. From that moment onwards, Eva and I got on like a house on fire.

Eva was one of the first cases I ever managed on my own. And as a young Social-Worker-in-training, I was not aware of how emotionally attached I could get to a service user. When a new service user comes along, not only do we invest our time and energy in them, we invest our hope, our love and a little of ourselves.

All the professionals who had worked with Eva before assured me that she would not stay with our service for more than a few weeks. The fact that Eva had no stability in her life seemed like a core problem to me, and so my main aim became trying to provide that stability. I did this by ensuring that our work together was based more on a critical friendship than on me playing the mother she did not have. Eva did not respond well to adults telling her what to do and so I wanted to be someone she could have honest discussions with. She began to see me as a big sister rather than a social worker and so I was able to tell her when I thought what she was doing was dangerous or wrong, and she would tell me whether she agreed with me (or whether I should piss off). In hindsight, building such a close relationship with Eva had damaging consequences for both of us – but at the time it kept her in a safe place for ten months; the longest and most stable placement she had had for years.

Eva and I worked together to get her her first educational qualifications; enrol her on a training course; sort her health problems; keep her out of trouble with the police; and manage the behaviour that was causing concern for the Sexual Exploitation Service. Eva made a lot of progress in those ten months and she was close to moving on positively from our service. She had six months to go before she would no longer need support from any service. However, with those six months to go, I had to leave the job I was doing to return to university.

We were taught about 'Relationship-Based Practice' and 'Endings Theory' in social work. But until you experience it for yourself, it is hard to realise the importance of managing your relationship with a service user. Even when you maintain your professional boundaries with a young person, it is all too easy for keywork sessions, after a practical task is completed, to become a long chat. And in those chats you can become further and further involved emotionally with your service user – wholly unintentionally. Even the most experienced social workers can find themselves more emotionally invested with a service user than they should be. It's an innocent, human reaction and often what drove us to do social work in the first place.

When I left my job Eva did not take it well. She refused to engage with any other workers. She seemed to think that any other worker couldn't possibly understand her like I did and she didn't want to start again from scratch.

When I returned back to the service a month later to say hi to everyone, one of the workers pulled me aside. They told me that Eva had left the service and was now a missing person. She was last reported being seen with a male that was known to be a sexual exploitation gang leader, and she was almost certainly homeless. The news broke my heart in a way I have never experienced before.

I can go days without thinking about Eva. Other nights I wake up in the middle of the night and just think about the work we did together; what I could have done differently; how I could have stopped this from happening; whether I should have stopped this from happening; wondering where she is now; wondering if she's okay; wondering if she's waiting for me to come and save her. Sometimes I get up and put a coat on, ready to go out and find her. But I don't know where she is. Or where to begin looking.

Every time I see a homeless person, I instantly think of her. Sometimes I sit and talk to that person; maybe to get rid of the guilt. Other times I walk home as quickly as possible and burst into tears.

Some people would say that you cannot let your job affect you this much. And as a result of my experiences of working with Eva I have worked hard to protect myself and young people from developing the same dependence. It was a painful and costly mistake, but one borne out of the desire to help.

Social workers, youth workers and community group workers are criticised, condemned, laughed at and even demonised, but what we do is hard and the things we encounter are traumatic. We fight causes that many others see as hopeless. We fight for a better society. We fight even though we know we cannot always win. We carry the burden that many in society fail to even recognise exists. And often we fail. Eva was not the first person to be let down and she will not be the last.

And that pain I feel about Eva, I know, is shared by many people I have trained and worked with. It makes you want to work harder; to study more and to reflect upon your practice so that you don't make the same mistake again.

Any professional who works with vulnerable and disaffected children will be quickly named, blamed and shamed for the smallest mistake. But we work in a challenging and risky environment and suffer enough without the vilification of the tabloid newspapers. Criticism from journalists is mere external noise to the guilt and pain you feel internally when you know you could have done something better. I cannot imagine the torment social workers who face serious case reviews go through when a child in their care dies. But I am sure that for the vast majority, their intention was good and like most youth and social workers, their motivation was to make a child's life better.

My Grandad always wanted me to be a barrister, but this job is challenging enough.

5 The riots

RESCUER

Eva was a major turning point in my social work journey. You may be asking yourself how I went from up-beat optimist to depressive pessimist in one paragraph, but that kind of reflects what it was like in reality. The transition was fast and unexpected. I felt that my attempt at being the Aunt Pat from Shy Keenan's book had failed. I began wondering if it was even possible to be an Aunt Pat as a social worker or whether the relationships I would form with service users would always have to be limited and conditional. These thoughts terrified me.

My placement was officially 100 days, however Poppy agreed to keep me on over the summer until term started again. As a paid employee I was given a larger case load with more complex cases. My case load dictated that I was dealing with sexual exploitation and drug addiction on a daily basis which was both soul-destroying and motivating. My desire to rescue people grew intensely as I built relationships with the service users, particularly Eva, who in hindsight reminded me somewhat of myself with her gobby stubbornness. The more deeply I understood the lives of the young people I was working with, the stronger my desire to make things better for them became. When you see someone every day, as I did Eva, you become unavoidably attached to them.

I began opening up to my supervisor about my unease about the relationship between social workers and service users being conditional. I wanted to be there for the young people 24 hours a day. The idea of talking to a young person who was in distress and who may need to call me at three in the morning did not seem like a chore but rather a service they deserved after being let down so monumentally by other adults in their life. Admitting this to my supervisor, however, quickly gained me the label 'Rescuer'. This was something that irritated me profusely, and still does to this day. And like all labels, it is something that I have had to work very hard to shake off.

Two years on, while I still carry that feeling of always wishing I could do more for service users, I now understand why it would be impossible to be a social worker 24 hours a day, seven days a week. As a young woman without children, I rarely have to put the needs of anybody else before my own. I can dedicate as much time as I want to work. My priorities, of course, would change entirely if I had children of my own. I also had very little insight into the incredibly damaging effects stress can have on your mental and physical health. I had absolutely no concept when I started social work of mindfulness, and needing mental space to process and recover from difficult cases. While I am still often criticised for living and breathing social work, I have learned some tough and important lessons about why having a work–life balance is essential. The cracks began showing in the summer of 2011.

BARE FLOORBOARDS AND BARE WALLS

As I was working longer than the 100 days that had been set for placement, I was able to support young people from when they arrived at our service until they were ready to move into their own first council house. The common goal for young homeless people who accessed our service was to get a council house. It soon became apparent to me that a poverty of wealth so easily leads to a poverty of aspiration. Almost all of the young people I worked with could not envisage themselves in private accommodation; it was too much money and in their eyes 'meant for posh people'.

There was no use in me encouraging these young people to dream bigger, to have faith in themselves, because frankly, even if they did want to rent a private flat, there simply was not the mechanism for them to achieve this. Landlords expect hundreds of pounds for a down-payment on top of the first month's rent. The young people I worked with could rarely find jobs, never mind have this amount of savings. And even if they did have a job, they were poorly paid and insecure. I began to understand and experience the sense of hopelessness that comes with being young and unemployed in this country.

The first time I moved a young man into his council property was the first time I saw a council house as it is given to new tenants. Put simply, if a private landlord was to present a flat to a private tenant in that condition, he would never be able to rent out the property. The place was disgusting. The floorboards were bare and worn. The wallpaper was peeling and stained. It was cold and small and devoid of all furniture including a cooker and a fridge. The gas was not connected and 20 or 30 unopened bills sat in the hallway for past tenants.

As an 18-year-old with our service, this was usually the ultimate goal they had been working towards; having their own place. Imagine the sheer disappointment when you realise that this cold and empty shell was the reality of that goal; that dream that you had been fighting for. If I was in their position I would seriously wonder what the point in trying was.

On a holiday to Paris with my Dad, I once found myself walking around a neighbourhood of cobbled streets, lined with tall, spacious, beautiful houses. Each one was different, with large windows and covered in climbing ivy. Between the houses were lush spots of plants and trees. The neighbourhood had been built as social housing at a time when the government saw a connection between a person's environment, nature and their wellbeing. It was exactly what housing should be like for all people. As I looked at the bare floorboards and bare walls of the English equivalent, I remember strongly feeling that council housing should not be like this. The young people I supported deserved a home to be proud of; somewhere they could feel safe and valued. Council housing wasn't their choice because they couldn't be bothered to save up for private accommodation. Council housing was a choice thrust upon them by unreasonably high rents and unfair minimum wages. The inequality and injustice of the situation for these young people was almost too hard to stomach.

THE RIOTS

In the summer of 2011 I was angry; really angry. I remember carrying a heavy weight with me. The combination of the poverty I had witnessed first-hand, and my sense of inner-turmoil with regard to my ability to help others, made me feel as if every incident of social injustice was a personal attack. The injustice of poverty was affecting people I knew; people I cared so much about.

I didn't sleep well during those last few weeks of summer. One night as I was watching 24-hour news at about 3am (as I tend to do when I cannot sleep), a news story broke of a huge fire in London. It wasn't clear initially what was happening until I accessed Twitter to find accounts of police brutality, a shooting and riots. I watched the riots unfold live on television for several hours until I fell asleep. When I woke up again at 8am, the unexplained images of fire and fighting now had an explanation.

The media spoke of *gangs* and *looting*, and showed London burning to the ground at the hands of *greedy hooligans*. If you relied purely on the news for an explanation of the riots you would naturally conclude that all the destruction had come about because people had suddenly and unpredictably become incredibly desperate for Nike trainers and flat screen TVs; almost like a zombie apocalypse where you wake up one morning to find everyone in desperate search of brains.

A few days after the rioting had broken out in Tottenham, as I walked home from work, I could sense an air of tension; of anger and hopelessness. Working in one of the city's most deprived communities, everyone was fully expecting riots to break out at any moment. Shops that were usually bustling with people were closing early and people were shuffling home with their heads down. The rioting had gripped the entire country and was the single event that inspired me to begin being more socially active. In particular, it was the following article by Wilkinson and Pickett, authors of *The Spirit Level* which propelled me into action:

> *If you're trying to explain the riots that started a year ago, the safest strategy is not to put all your eggs in one basket but to come up with a long list of contributory factors ... We need to join up the dots and think about the causes of these causes.*

> *None of these things crop up by chance, quite unrelated to one another.... The truth is that just as tobacco is a physiological poison, Britain's high levels*

of inequality are a social poison that increases the risks of a wide range of social ills...

But how does this social poison work? It makes some people look as if they are worth much more than others; not just a little bit more, but anything from supremely important to almost worthless. Money becomes the measure of personal worth.

Basically, antisocial societies cause antisocial behaviour. Greater inequality weakens community life, trust gives way to status competition, family life suffers, children grow up prepared for a dog-eat-dog world, class divisions and prejudices are strengthened and social mobility slows. If consumerism helps bolster the increasingly strained sense of self-worth even of those on above average incomes, how do you deal with the sense of worthlessness that comes with youth unemployment and a job seekers' allowance of only £56 a week?

–Richard Wilkinson and Kate Pickett, www.theguardian.com/
commentisfree/2012/aug/05/riots-inequality-poverty-self-esteem

I knew from my own experience that everything Wilkinson and Pickett said was true. I could not cope, however, with the anger I felt when people who did not work with the disaffected, live in the areas they live in, or have any experiential knowledge of them, felt they could diagnose the cause of the riots as being purely down to greed and a mob-mentality. When a doctor, trained in the workings of the human body, diagnoses a person, it is rare that the diagnosis is challenged with such contempt as that a social scientist would receive. For when a social scientist, who is an expert in the way humans react in their environments and with each other, highlights particular patterns which may point to a cause, people feel able to entirely ignore that knowledge and expertise. It seems everyone views themselves as an expert in sociology. My frustration convinced me that I needed to let people know about the expertise social workers have. How I was going to do that, I wasn't quite sure.

THE DAY OWEN JONES CHANGED MY LIFE

Books change your life. I remember vividly the first time I found a book so engrossing that it transported me to another time and place. It was *All Quiet on the Western Front* by Erich Maria Remarque.

I was lying on my Grandad's bed. It had been a month since my Grandad, who I called Dumper (and still to this day don't know why), had passed away. I remember being curled up in the heavy quilted bed sheets and I couldn't shake my sense of loss. I began reading the small and unassuming book. There is a moment in it, towards the end, where Paul Bäumer, the lead character, who is a soldier in World War I, kills an enemy soldier. After killing his enemy, Bäumer is overwhelmed by his actions. He talks desperately to the corpse:

Comrade, I did not want to kill you…But you were only an idea to me before, an abstraction that lived in my mind and called forth its appropriate response. It was that abstraction I stabbed. But now, for the first time, I see you are a man like me.

When I closed that book I felt disoriented. For the hours I was reading it, I was not aware of the heavy quilts, the heat pouring from the unnecessary electric fire, or the absence of my Grandad. I was so embedded in the mind and conscience of Paul Bäumer. His conversation with the corpse resonated with so many of humanity's failings.

All too late do we realise that those we see as our enemy – asylum seekers, drug addicts, benefit scroungers, criminals – are not in fact some abstract monsters, but rather human beings, like ourselves. If more people saw the actual person rather than the label that surrounds them, I truly believe we would be a step closer toward Utopia.

There are also those books which change your life, not because you become engrossed in a character, but because they crystallise perfectly something you knew deep down to be true and yet had never been able to articulate.

A month before the riots broke out I had decided to do my dissertation on the demonisation of the working class. I happily told my Mum about my choice of topic and quickly found my idea crushed to the ground as she informed me that a book, with that very title, had just been released. Who was this bastard who had stolen my dissertation, I wondered. I quickly bought his book and began reading with skepticism. It didn't take me long to realise that Owen Jones's *Chavs: The Demonization of the Working Class*, was infinitely better than any attempt I would have made.* With elegance and ferocity, Owen highlighted the unjustifiable scorn that poorer people receive in this country, and its devastating consequences.

While my evidence of demonisation would have boiled down to Jenny at the job centre being mean to one of my young people because they were wearing a tracksuit, Owen had clearly done his research. He pointed out under-reported but important facts such as the £16 billion worth of benefits that was going unclaimed every year while Gordon Brown spoke of benefit scroungers and saving money; the £16 billion equalling two-and-a-half times the money the government was trying to save. Owen highlighted the hypocrisy of

---

* It's probably worth nothing that my admiration for Owen Jones has taken a rather unhealthy turn. Last year, when on a bus in Manchester, I saw Owen standing outside Rossiter's Restaurant. With all the dignity of a screaming banshee I ordered the bus driver to stop immediately and practically threw myself off a moving vehicle. I fumbled desperately for my phone and called my best friend, who shares my admiration (I refuse to use the word obsession). She directed me to breathe and stay calm. I looped the restaurant so as to give the impression I was just casually walking by. As I passed him I did the most embarrassingly unconvincing, *Oh, are you Owen Jones?* It was obvious from the tremor in my voice that I knew full well who he was and was a big fan. Luckily for me, Owen turned out to be a charming man. Unluckily for him, it has increased my obsession. I mean admiration.

a government which focuses all of its energy on clamping down on a small proportion of welfare cheats, while turning a blind eye to the billions that is lost through tax evasion. He provided statistics to prove that having a job in Britain is not a sure fire way of escaping poverty. *Chavs* provided the statistics and research to explain why the young people I worked with were experiencing so much injustice.

The paragraph that really stood out to me was a prediction of what may happen if Britain continued to allow its society to be so unequal, and if it failed to instate a new class politics. Owen writes: *It would be tempting to make all sorts of doom-laden, apocalyptic predictions about what will happen if such a movement fails to get off the ground, and warn darkly of riots and revolutions* (p. 268). And of course, a month later, England was plagued by riots.

Watching them unfold on television and hearing the vile words spoken about communities just like the one I worked in made me so angry. I don't remember a time before that when I had ever felt so furious with Britain. My experience of the deprived community I worked with was a largely positive one and I needed to stand up for what I believed in. My role as a social worker had to be more than helping one person at a time. I believe social workers need to have a voice and advocate for those communities who need it most.

6 The key to being a good social worker is good rum and a great friend

THE IMPORTANCE OF SOCIAL MEDIA

Why don't you write a blog? These words came from my friend Ben's mouth when he was clearly sick of me relaying my anger and frustration about the injustices of the world to him. It was clear to those who knew me best that social work was changing me. For better or for worse, it was all I could talk about. It had consumed me.

There were so many questions I needed answering about what the role of a social worker was. Do we comply with systems we know to be unfair and corrupt? Or do we challenge those systems knowing it could put the service user in a difficult situation? For example, how could I challenge a staff member from the Job Centre who was being incredibly rude to my service user without it costing the service user their housing benefits? My head was a mess.

I began blogging that summer. I was, and still remain, a complete failure when it comes to computers and the internet. I gained quite a reputation at university for losing hundreds of pages of essays and dissertations because I didn't know how to back up my work. In fact, if this book gets to print in one piece it will be a minor miracle. The idea of using an internet-based blog was, to my friends, fairly hilarious. However, I managed to master the basics, along with Twitter, and began venting my thoughts and frustrations to the world. Or, to no one at all, as it would turn out for the first few weeks.

I never began blogging with the intention of having an audience. Like I said, there were things I needed to get off my chest. I never really expected anyone to reply. After my first post, however, I found blogging to be an amazing form of stress management. I've never been one for keeping a diary, but in some ways, this is what I was doing.

Another part of me wanted the people closest to me to understand what I did, and why. A lot of my friends and family knew very little about social work and it was important to me (if not them) that they understood the reality of what I do. I publicised my first few blogs on Twitter and Facebook and got kind and helpful responses. The more people read it, the more blogging became a form of national and international supervision. People from Thailand and the United States of America were offering me their insights into the problems I had posed. It opened a whole new world of social work to me.

I believe online blogging has the potential to be to our generation what pamphleteering was to the Reformation. Pamphleteering played a central role in allowing Martin Luther to challenge the hegemony of the Roman Catholic Church, eventually leading to the

Protestant Reformation. A blog is a forum where an individual can discuss any topic they like – and in a nation where 33 million people use the internet daily, it is possible to reach a huge audience within seconds. The power of online media should not be underestimated.

Social media opened up so many doors for me. I still find my online journey quite overwhelming. One October morning I was approached by *The Guardian*, via Twitter, and asked if I wanted to write a piece for their Social Care Network. I almost fell out of my seat. It had been a dream of mine since the age of 11 to write for a national newspaper. And as a lover of all things left-wing, *The Guardian* was predictably my favourite paper. Since my first article appeared online, I have been offered numerous opportunities to write about my profession and ultimately it led to me writing the book you are reading now. (So, if you want to blame anyone for this book, blame the internet.)

Social media has enabled me to advocate for my service users and my profession on a national level. That need I had felt for my role as a social worker to be more than helping one person at a time, was, and still is, being met. I don't pretend to think that my writing is changing the way Britain views social work, but I do hope that one day it will. And at present, I enjoy being a small voice in a big debate.

HERE IS THE THREE-HUNDREDTH PHOTO OF WHAT I HAD FOR DINNER

While I am on the subject of social media, I can't help but have a little rant about a pet hate of mine. There is a tendency among those of a younger generation (and, yes, I am classing myself in that generation) to make sure that they are not seen as caring too much about anything. It's almost as if caring about things isn't fashionable. I am aware that I sound like my grandparents when I say this, but I do believe it to be true. A prime example is the 'Political Facebook' status. If an individual posts a status up about Thatcherism, feminism or the Welfare State, they are seen by many as a bore. My partner was once told by a friend that he needed to *lay off the serious stuff on Facebook* as it can get *a bit embarrassing*. Well, I'm sorry, but I would rather have 200 Facebook statuses promoting discussion and debate about a whole range of issues – even if I did not agree with a single one of them and they made my blood boil – than have to look at one more picture of what someone had for dinner with the caption *Nom nom nom* underneath it.

I'm not 'political' in a bid to be cool or fashionable; I'm political because some things are too important not to talk about. And just as I will bore you in the pub about the travesty that is homelessness in Britain, so will I bore you on Facebook. Because ignoring an issue is as good as exacerbating it. One of my favourite quotations of all time is: *In the end, we will remember not the words of our enemies, but the silence of our friends.*

It is of course up to you what you use your Facebook for. Some people find it useful to have as a space where they can just keep in contact with family and friends, and it's important to have private spheres where you don't feel the need to fight a cause. However, I suggest that if you are one of the many who have several hundred friends, that you use your online presence to make a difference. Facebook is a fantastic platform for creating social change; don't be embarrassed to use it to stand up for social work.

THEN I FOUND LOUISE

When I was younger I imagined university to be a place where people met up in coffee shops or pubs after class and discuss all the issues that mattered to them. It may be because I had read *The Women's Room* too many times that I had the false expectation of people excitedly gathering together to dissect social topics with academic rigour, but I genuinely was slightly confused when I arrived as an undergraduate to find that students' social time was mainly spent playing sport or drinking. There are, of course, exceptions to this rule; however it simply wasn't seen as acceptable to discuss poverty in the pub, as you would be blamed for bringing everyone on a bit of a downer. For that reason I found my first degree somewhat underwhelming. I didn't hold high expectations for my Masters being any different.

Then I found Louise.

I met Louise on the Social Work Masters course interview day for the University of Sheffield. There were four of us, all women, awkwardly spaced out around the waiting room. It was one of those situations where you are all united by the impending, horrifying experience of an interview. However, you simultaneously find yourself judging these people, as ultimately they are your competition. The classic awkward conversation began between strangers: *You nervous?*

As soon as I turned to ask Louise the same question I had asked the other three women, we immediately did a double-take. *Do I know you?* we both asked. To this day we still cannot work out if we'd met before, but somehow we were both very familiar to each other.

Louise had studied philosophy as an undergraduate at the University of Sheffield. She had taken a year out to work in Borneo and had taken an entirely different route into social work from me. Talking about social work and social justice was not 'work' or 'study' for Louise. It is her genuine passion. Like all exceptional social workers, Louise cannot turn off the care she has for other human beings. When something needs to be challenged, Louise is never afraid to stand up for what she believes. Numerous times have I been with Louise at a party or a meal, when someone has used discriminatory language. I remember one particular incident where the term 'smack-head' was used to describe the people accessing the local methadone clinic. Louise was ferocious in her defence; not only on behalf of those against whom the term discriminated, but also for the ideals she held for a fair and equal society.

It was exciting finding someone who wanted to talk about social issues, not just during university time, but also in their spare time. At least three times a week we would meet up to go to our favourite Greek deli and hypothesise about our day on placement. The owner must have made a killing selling halloumi to us two. It was clear that Louise and I shared the same core values about human rights and person-centred practice. Our different backgrounds meant, however, that we had different approaches to similar problems. Louise's philosophy degree encouraged me to think about my cases in a way I had never fathomed before.

One particular discussion with Louise stands out for me. It was at a party, fairly late on in the evening, when we tried to ascertain why social work was necessary in society. The discussion strayed onto the question of how you define good and bad. Social work is wholly reliant on the idea that we create positive change for people. But again, what is 'positive change'? Society is based on so many man-made rules that we now hold to be self-evident, such as 'killing is wrong' and 'child abuse is wrong'. While I fully agree with these statements, they are still only an opinion. There is no definitive, unchallengeable force (unless you are religious) which states that these things are a fact. Therefore, why is my opinion more valid than someone who may think that child abuse is not wrong. Because child abuse causes harm? Again, who is to say that harm is something that humans should avoid? One of the best things I have learned from a training course is that *we do not know if we hold the truth*.

I spent the next few weeks asking everyone I knew why they think harm and neglect is bad. Many people saw it as an obvious question and wouldn't entertain answering it. Other people grasped the complexity of how society defines good and evil. If you think on a macro level about how society structures itself and how we define good and bad, I guarantee you will find yourself on a never-ending spiral of doubt and confusion. But it's always good to ask yourself these questions once in a while. Like when you look up to the stars on a clear night and realise just how insignificant your little life is.

Becoming close to my course mate Louise was, without a doubt, central to my development as a social worker. Empathy is an essential skill as a social worker. However, when a service user you work with has experienced a particularly upsetting incident, and one which, if a few small things had been different, may not have happened, it creates an overwhelming sense of anger within you. A good cure for that anger was always texting Louise. Once I'd texted Louise about the cause of my stress I could guarantee receiving within minutes a text back with an equal magnitude of anger.

I cannot recommend peer-supervision enough. You can find a strength in peer-supervision which is difficult to obtain elsewhere. On a Friday night, after a few rums, you can talk for hours about everything that has happened that week. You can tell them, with such honesty, all the thoughts you had, which maybe your supervisor would not understand, and know that they will listen and be honest back. I found in Louise an individual with an inspiring yet intimidating intellect, who was as passionate about this profession as I was; and it gave me so much hope.

THE DISSERTATION

Second year started and my dissertation loomed over me. Since Owen Jones had stolen my idea, I was even more pressed for a topic. The best piece of advice I was given was to do it on something I really cared about. That way, even when it gets tough, you will have a clear purpose for completing it. The answer was simple; I would do it on Eva.

I knew next to nothing about sexual exploitation before I had met Eva. Exploitation was a topic that dominated Eva's life and I had learned a little through sexual exploitation conferences and advocating for her with the local prevention service. Before I began reading for my dissertation, I didn't think there was anything wrong with using the term 'child prostitution'. The beautiful thing about social work is the more you read, the more you discover the inherent prejudices, assumptions and biases that exist in everyday language. 'Child prostitute' implied that the young person being used for sex was in some way a willing participant. Many would see this as political correctness gone mad. I couldn't disagree more.

My dissertation gave me an excellent opportunity to explore theories about the language we use. Language is extremely powerful and easily creates and maintains power imbalances. While we continue to call young people who have offended 'young offenders' we will continue to see them as nothing more than criminals. The label defines them and leaves room for no other aspects of their personality. Society loves labels, and sometimes these labels are necessary in order to ensure people gain access to the right services. For example, it is no use offering transgender support services to someone who is not transgender. There simply aren't the resources to offer all services to all people. I like the fact that it is part of our job as social workers to make sure these labels are fit for purpose.

Knowing how Eva had reacted to the Sexual Exploitation Service, and knowing how she viewed her relationship with the person that professionals believed to be exploiting her, it seemed obvious to me that my focus should be on relationship-based practice. Not that I knew anything about relationship-based practice until my university supervisor told me that this theory would relate perfectly to my 'Rescuer' tendencies. Like most things my supervisor said, she was completely right. I read as much as I could around the topic of relationship-based practice and began to realise that the things that came so naturally to me, and were my strengths as a practitioner, were aspects of theory. Empathy, for example, was a tool that could be analysed, reflected upon and refined to make me a better practitioner. I had found a theory that really spoke about the sort of social worker I wanted to be.

Eva was in love with her exploiter. He was her boyfriend and nothing anyone could say would change that. I fell in love as a teenager and remember thinking, well, how on earth do you combat teenage love? These musings led to the following blog:

Teenage kicks

In case I haven't made it clear, I am currently working on a dissertation. It's on the role of relationship-based social work practice in helping sexually exploited young people. The reading aspect is fascinating. It really is. And the writing aspect… well, that would be fun if, you know, books and television and the internet and the act of staring at a blank wall had not been invented. I am a procrastinator extraordinaire.

It has become clear to me that our current political and professional understanding of sexual exploitation is, to put it frankly, a bit of a mess. If it weren't for the tireless work of charitable organisations such as the National Working Group, Barnardo's, ECPAT and CEOP, to name a few, I imagine we would still be calling it 'child prostitution' and assuming it happened to one in a million girls. Or, our knowledge would stem from recent media interest in the subject and we would all be certain (much like we are all certain that benefit fraud is the downfall of this country) that sexual exploitation involves gangs of Asian men raping young white girls; girls whose parents are terribly irresponsible for letting them out of the house past six at night. Luckily, I don't think this fallacy has seeped into the public consciousness just yet. But we should not rest easy. While Tim Loughton and Sue Berelowitz try and get the story straight over the next 18 months, there is a particular complexity that I would like to ponder with you.

When I was 17, I fell in love. Hopelessly, stupidly, head-over-heels in love. With a man who I had spoken to once. I used to work in a Chinese take-away – and when I say work, I mean sit at a till for five hours and get people's orders wrong. (My boss told me, when I left after two years to go to university, that I was the most useless employee he had ever had and he'd only kept me on as I made him laugh. I still haven't decided if that's a good or a bad thing.) So, one evening, I was 'working', and in walked a tall, handsome, twenty-something, Irish-looking, dream of a man. He asked for a chicken chow mein. I got the order wrong. We laughed. It was like something out of a Jane Austen novel. And so the infatuation began.

From then on I came up with cunning and imaginative ways to find out all the information I could about this man – his name, his job, his shoe size – and ultimately marry him. Once I searched through a takeaway bin for 40 minutes to find the order sheet which had his mobile number on. That's all the dignity I had managed to amass in my 17 years of existence. If I had put as much effort into my A-levels as I did in stalking this man, who knows where I'd be now. I could have been Queen of Everything.

Luckily for me, this man, who was ten years my senior, was level-headed enough to consider me too young to be a potential girlfriend. It turns out my subtle flirting had actually not been subtle. Who'da thunk?! However, if he had decided that I could be his girlfriend, I am pretty sure I would have done anything for that man. I'm pretty sure I still would. I've been in love since, but as a teenage mass of hormones/emotion he will always remain in my memory as perfection personified. And I'm not the only teenage girl who has temporarily ignored any elements of self-respect or logic in pursuit of a man. I have a similar story for every one of my female friends. We all went to good schools. We all have degrees. It's just how most teenage girls are (and that's coming from a strident feminist!)

Which got me thinking. I have been lucky enough to only ever be in relationships with lovely, caring males. I have never fallen in love with someone who has wanted to hurt me or use me. As an adult, I can say that if I was in an abusive or exploitative relationship now, I would be able to defend myself and walk away. I can say that, but I can never really know as I have not experienced it. But when I think back to my teenage years, I do not know what would have been if I had met the wrong person. I had bags of self-esteem, was a notoriously fierce feminist and thought I knew what a 'bad' relationship looked like. But if a man, a man like ChineseTakeawayIrishDream Man (as my friends refer to him) had spent years building what I thought was a loving and caring relationship with me, I imagine there is a way that I too could have become another sexually exploited young person. If he began subtly, and convinced me to do a few small things that I felt were 'wrong' in order to help him or to get him out of trouble, such as picking up an unmarked package; and if he kept me believing that he did love me, then things could very easily spiral. I'd like to think that I would have had enough support to escape the abuse, but then I think, would I have even recognised it as abuse at all!

The term 'sexual exploitation' implies a powerless victim; an 'exploitee' who has been abused and manipulated by an 'exploiter'. The reality, however, can be very different. My experience in working with sexually exploited young people has demonstrated that, often, the young person who is on the 'exploitation register' is not powerless, but rather makes a choice to have sex with dangerous (and numerous) men. Academics Chase and Statham argue that the choice these young people make is a constrained one, but I do not yet know how we begin to break those constraints. Male exploiters who pose as 'the boyfriend' are experts at what they do. They spend years building up a relationship with a young person because they know how powerful that bond can be. How do we help young people to make an 'unconstrained choice' without imposing our own values and ideals?

If a teenage girl (or boy), who may be a lot younger than 17, is in love with a man who is sexually exploiting her, we as social workers have an almighty task. We can work to empower that young person, provide self-esteem classes, encourage education and training, sort housing and liaise with police to deal with the exploiter. But what do we do if that young person chooses to keep going back to her exploiter because she loves him? Any social worker who is willing to take on teenage love is a braver (or possibly dumber) person than I am.

If anyone knows where to start, I would love to hear from you.

It is interesting reading this blog back, as sexual exploitation has recently gained a lot of media attention due to the activities of grooming gangs in Derby, Rotherham and Oxford. As a result, it seems that the news is purporting the idea of it being a crime purely perpetrated by Asian men. It is not. Nor is it only young girls who are being exploited. What remains clear to me is that Britain does not yet have the resources to be able to effectively prevent and tackle this terrible crime.

STREET-WISE GRANNIES

The dissertation process was a long one. I began to realise that there are many ways to develop in social work, and that research and academia were another route to helping people. That is of course if you are good at research and academia. Mine was not the academic route. But realising this was useful in terms of deciding what my strengths indeed were. I am a practical social worker who luckily had Louise, who was an academic, to help me understand methodologies.

Being able to understand, analyse and critique complex theories though is, in my opinion, an integral part of being a good social worker. There is an ongoing debate (mainly among people who aren't qualified social workers) as to whether you have to be 'book smart' to be a social worker or whether you have to have good people skills. It's simple; you have to have both. And the two aren't mutually exclusive. There is this myth that exists that people who are able to obtain a university degree are unable to communicate with those who haven't. It goes hand-in-hand with the assumption that everyone who goes to university is middle class. As someone who was eligible for the highest tier of Education Maintenance Allowance at school, and who received full government funding at university due to high grades and low income, this assumption is something I find quite offensive. That said, I do believe it is imperative that more is done to ensure university education is accessible to low-income families. Social work would benefit from this especially.

While we need to keep away from social work the elitism that has plagued many other professions, we cannot pretend that a high level of training and intellect is not needed in order to do our job well. We work with some of the most complex and damaged human beings who need expert intervention if they are to have any hope of a positive future. It seems so obvious to me that the best minds should go into facing the challenges of child abuse, sexual exploitation, youth crime and Mental Health Services. These problems are too important not to be taken seriously. Society deserves a high standard of social services, and I am positive that there are plenty of people out there who would make fantastic social workers if they were given the right incentives and opportunities to become one.

This relates to another question I frequently get asked as a young social worker: *So, what real life experience do you have?* This question makes me die inside a little every time I hear it. Nonetheless, I usually manage to maintain good social etiquette and answer with something along the lines of: *Well that depends what you mean by real life experience.* I am confident that while ageing will naturally bring insight into various aspects of the human lifespan, it is not essential that social workers be old in order to be good at their job. But I would say that wouldn't I?

I could write a whole other book on the experience I have gained growing up in one of Britain's most deprived seaside towns, and how my family shaped my desire to do social work – but frankly, it's nobody's business but mine. While I know that I had a lot of challenges thrown at me at a young age, which enables me to relate to many of the young people I work with, I don't think that my 'life experience' alone would make me a good social worker.

Life experience is only beneficial if you have been able to process it, recover from it and relate it to practice in a positive and objective way. That is not an easy task and it is common for professionals to think that just because they have been depressed in the past, that means they understand everything about a service user who is suffering from depression now. That is an unhelpful and dangerous mistake to make and reinforces Virginia Bottomley's assertion that social workers are nothing more than 'street-wise grannies'. Along with life experience has to come an in-depth knowledge of tools for intervention and an ability to constantly reflect on the actions you choose to take, what you believe as well as what you think and why you think it. Deep critical reflection is a skill and an art-form, and not one that comes naturally to anybody.

7 Red tape

A STATUTORY PLACEMENT

Alright, kid. The call came from Declan, a man who I had met numerous times during my volunteering time with young people who offend. *You can guess what this call is about*, he said. My second placement was to be with the Youth Justice Service. While Youth Justice was clearly my major passion, I would be lying if I said I wasn't slightly disappointed that I didn't get a child protection position. I really wanted the challenge, and felt I knew most of what there was to know about Youth Justice. Of course, as usual, I was completely wrong.

My supervisor for the placement was Phil, another person who I knew very well. Phil had seen me working on my first placement as we both supported the same young man. I wasn't sure whether it was a good or a bad thing to have someone who knew me well, but I was willing to give it a try.

The first few weeks were spent trying to navigate my way round the Criminal Justice System and sentencing. What Orders were given for which offences and what the young people had to do to successfully complete an Order. I had to remember supervision requirements, elcotronic tagging, breach processes; the difference between Youth Rehabilitation Orders and Detention and Training Orders. The list goes on, but I don't want to bore you with detail. Nor do I want to frustrate myself by realising I don't remember half the stuff I was taught. The amount of technical and legal information I had to absorb in that week was fairly overwhelming. Luckily, Phil was very patient with me and made me write down *everything* that he said to me.

Statutory placement really focuses the mind. I was anxious to ensure that my interventions were based in theory. Unlike voluntary placement, I didn't feel automatically confident in what I was doing. The legal aspect of statutory work meant the details of past Serious Case Reviews were swirling around my head. I was very aware that I was making big decisions with big consequences. I began to struggle with the power:

Gollum, the social worker

I appreciate that this blog is at risk of becoming a monthly discussion of why Lord of the Rings *is so ridiculously great (swoons at the thought of Legolas), but there is a good reason why I am referring to it again, I promise.*

A few weeks ago I was bed-ridden due to flu. A flu that my partner quickly learned was much worse than any flu anybody else had ever had. *So bad in fact that,* you couldn't possibly understand what I'm going through *and actually* it's lucky that I have such a high pain threshold because most people wouldn't cope with **this** flu. *(It was just normal flu and no, I didn't win an Oscar.) My poor partner, therefore had to come up with a plan to put either me, or himself, out of our misery. Luckily, he chose to buy me a tub of Ben and Jerry's ice cream and rent the* Lord of the Rings *trilogy on DVD. Watching Aragorn, Legolas and Gimli tirelessly trekking across Middle Earth in order to defend all that is good and true is enough to stop anyone wallowing in their own self-pity.*

During this viewing, however, I felt a sense of unease. A feeling that I had not experienced in my previous 800 viewings. Obviously, my support was behind the fellowship. But also, I felt an odd affinity with Gollum. What was it about this isolated little river dweller that had me so troubled?

Of course! Gollum is like a social worker.

Now before any social workers close this book or send me abuse (Yeah?! Well you look like that fat hobbit at the start!), it has nothing to do with physical appearance. Nor his preference for eating raw fish. No. Gollum is like a social worker because he, like us, has a daily struggle with 'power'.

Social workers are faced with some of the most difficult decisions any professional has to make. Deciding when, or if, to admit a person to a psychiatric ward, or whether or not to take a child away from their family, are the most overt examples of the power social workers possess. But our power is not always overt. It is often a lot more subtle and lies in our influence, persuasion and expertise. Even when we think that we are 'working with' a service user to achieve their goals, the context itself places power with the social worker. If someone is in contact with a social worker it means they need help with something; be it finding housing, addressing an addiction or adopting a child. Most social workers enter the profession wanting to help in this way, and therefore, from the outset, we assume that we have some power; power to help. The minute social work professionals stop recognising that their position comes with an inherent power, then their practice becomes incredibly dangerous.

Gollum is so consumed by the ring and the power it possesses that he cannot see that it is destroying him, and for social workers too, power can be very destructive. If we do not constantly analyse and re-evaluate our practice, values and beliefs, we risk not treating each service user as an individual. I have seen in work with sexually exploited young people how formulaic tools and procedures are put in place to help the young person, when actually they ignore that young person's wishes, feelings, resilience; their individuality. Decisions are made on behalf of sexually exploited young people, often against their will, which further isolates them and increases feelings of low self-worth. Even my social worker doesn't listen to me. *If there is disagreement, we must always ask ourselves why we think our view of how to live is better than our service users', and what gives us the right to make decisions on behalf of others. Using our power thoughtlessly will destroy our ability to help.*

There are obviously areas where the analogy of Gollum as social worker does not fit, and you could argue that I should have gone down the Spider-Man route of with great power comes great responsibility. *I am not asserting that the service user is powerless, or that social workers obsess about gaining power. Nor does power have to be a bad thing. The point is that if social workers do not constantly critique, analyse and review the power-play in their interactions with service users, colleagues, managers and other agencies, our practice can become quite destructive. But what does give social workers the right to make decisions on behalf of others, especially if they disagree with us? The law is often an ass, so answering 'legal powers' doesn't answer the philosophical aspect of it.*

Seeking some sort of clarity, I went to see my personal tutor. A woman so wise that you instantly feel twice as clever just by being in the same room as her. We had a long, long discussion about the role of power; the theories, faces, contradictions, problems… the list went on. I talked. I listened. I even felt brave enough to challenge her. It was a fantastic discussion. And her conclusion? Her wise parting words that would send me on my way into the big, scary world of social work? If you're not in a constant state of confusion, you're not doing it right.

Of course, as you develop in social work, that confusion comes with more confidence, but it is important to always remember the lesson: We do not know that we hold the truth.

ADAM

One of the first cases I was given was a young boy called Adam. Adam was on bail after he had committed several burglaries in the space of a few days. The court gave him an intensive programme to follow, which meant he had to come into the office several times a week to see me and had to be in education for 25 hours each week. As he was new to the service it seemed like a good, simple case to start me off with.

Adam's situation turned out to be much more complicated than anyone could have anticipated.

My first interview with Adam was a confusing one. He walked into the small interview room at the Youth Justice Service looking somewhat puzzled as to who I was and why he had been directed to come to this building. I carefully explained who I was and what Order the court had given him, and why. I asked him if he understood and had any questions. He understood. I then talked to him a bit about himself. Adam was a small and very skinny boy. He wore a black tracksuit, black cap and red bandana in his trouser waist. I knew from my previous placement that there was a local postcode gang who were notorious for wearing red bandanas. As I had known this boy less than five minutes, I didn't think it would be wise for me, a white woman, to accuse him, a black boy, of being in a gang, so I subtly asked about his associates. He didn't give much away. What he did tell me was that he had numerous siblings, one of whom had moved to Pakistan to go and work. Adam became quite animated when telling me that he was a top footballer who had been selected for the county team. Adam was sweet and presented as much younger than 14. I told him to come in the next day to see me at the same time.

The next day I waited. There was no sign of Adam. Three hours later, Adam casually sauntered into the office and decided to scream abuse at the reception staff. By the time I got downstairs Adam was sitting quietly. I couldn't quite believe the reports I was hearing from the receptionist. How could this little boy have been as vicious as they were saying?

I questioned Adam and he responded very calmly that he had shouted because they had been racist. When I probed him further he told me that they hadn't said anything racist, but he could see it in their eyes. This would turn out to be a recurring theme in many of Adam's offences. When a shopkeeper refused to serve cigarettes to Adam, he was certain it was because of the colour of his skin and not because he was underage.

I asked Adam why he had been late. He shrugged. *Can you tell the time okay?* I inquired. He shrugged again. Adam soon revealed, aged 14, he could not read, write or tell the time. I needed to know more about this boy.

I established that he had a social worker and missing person's worker. I began gathering as much information I could about Adam and his family. During my research, social services told me that Adam's brother was in India, not Pakistan, as Adam had said. There was a report of Adam's brother being locked in his room by the father for three days. The father was not charged, but shortly after the incident the brother was sent abroad. I was worried. I arranged to meet the family.

THE DIFFERENCE BETWEEN TRANSLATION AND INTERPRETING

I arrived outside Adam's family home. It was the bottom flat of a small council block. The curtains, closed during the day, were tied up with string. The parents invited me in. They were not happy to see me and the interpreter. The father was a very elderly man who clearly had a chest infection of some sort, as he coughed loud and hard between sentences. The mother looked 30 years younger than her husband and appeared very nervous. Neither spoke English. In all honesty, my first impression of Adam's father was marred by the abuse he was suspected of having inflicted upon his son. I tried my best to keep an open mind as I interviewed him about his family.

Conversations were long and frustrating. I would say my piece and it would be interpreted for five minutes. I always thought it was odd that it would take five minutes to translate something I had said in 30 seconds. I assumed that was the nature of their home language. We tried to ascertain where Adam's older brother was. The family wouldn't give us an address. The father only stated that he had sent his son because he was annoyed with him getting into trouble. After our first meeting I was worried for Adam's safety. If they had sent Adam's brother away to some untraceable address, then maybe they would do the same to Adam.

The next week Adam went missing. He had always run away a lot, but only for a few days. This time he was gone for weeks. A multi-agency meeting was held with social services and the police. Piecing together the information we had received from the parents, there was serious concern that they had sent Adam abroad. We needed to find Adam's passport.

The next meeting I attended at the family home was extremely fraught. The translator explained to the family that the police needed to see Adam's passport to ensure he was still in the country and still safe. The mother, who had been very quiet in all other meetings, began screaming at us. She refused to give us his passport. I was convinced at this point that Adam was abroad. I left the house feeling very low. Something was bothering me about this case. Seeing Adam's mother so distressed was upsetting, but also her distress did not seem like a mother who knew where her son was.

I sought supervision from my all-knowing supervisor, who taught me something which would transform the entire case. She told me that interpretation is not the same as translation. When working with people who cannot speak English, there is so much room for misunderstanding. She told me to ask the interpreter to translate everything word for word. It would take longer, but things would become clearer.

Two days later I went back to see the mother and father. We began with new ground rules about how things would be translated. The parents agreed and translation began. After two hours, my view of the family had been transformed. The mother explained to me that she did not understand the systems in this country. Good multi-agency working is essential to successful safeguarding of children. Every serious case review reminds us of the need for all professionals, be it social workers, police, teachers, or youth workers, to talk to each other all the time. Adam's case naturally attracted a lot of professionals. There were five core professionals who ended up meeting once a fortnight due to the frequent increases in risk as Adam continued to go missing and engage in criminal activity. She did not know why so many people were coming to her house, or what was happening.

When I slowly translated to Adam's parents what my role was, and why we had asked for the passport, the father explained that in his own country the police were not to be trusted. He had locked Adam's brother in a room and sent him abroad because the police were coming to the house a lot looking for him. The father was scared for his son. Two hours of honest and clarifying conversation resulted in the start of a trusting relationship; the first that family had had with a professional. Adam's mother disappeared upstairs and returned with a small book in her hand. It was Adam's passport. *Please find my son*, she begged.

THE START OF SOMETHING

Adam eventually returned home. Having built up a better relationship with his family, I had a clearer understanding of his life. This made providing support for Adam infinitely easier. The professional relationship I built up with Adam was a powerful one. It enabled me to calm him down when he became violent; encourage him to attend education and provide him with somewhere to go when he needed help.

Adam and I were completely different. We had grown up in different countries with different cultures. He always laughed when I complained it was too hot. He told me I would *die if I went to Dubai*. I'm sure he was right. Unfortunately, Adam spent his fifteenth birthday in prison. I went to visit him a week later and noticed the card I had sent had prime position in the centre of his desk.

While Adam has not yet been able to stop offending, I hope that his experience with me taught him that he could trust professionals and white people. And hopefully it led to him letting other professionals into his life to provide him with the help he needs and deserves.

There's a time and a place for Parka coats

The social work course has a large practical element. I'm very glad it does as it teaches you things that you would never learn from a book; such as not wearing a Parka coat to court.

Journalist? the security guard asked me as I entered court.

No. Youth Justice worker, I replied with a degree of authority.

If you can empty your pockets into this tray and step through the detector, please.

Now, this is where I learned the valuable lesson of NEVER wearing a Parka coat to court. Here is a list of the contents of my pockets. My many, many, many pockets:

Four pens (all blue)

A phone

An iPod

Three packs of tissues

Reams and reams of mindless scribbles on scraps of paper

Lip balm

Deodorant

Eight leaflets on homelessness

Socks

A golf visor (I have never played golf in my life)

A handbook on The UN Convention on the Rights of the Child

A BOUNCY BALL

...and, of course, a red bra.

There was plenty more in my pockets, but before I had finished the security guard stopped me (probably because he wanted to spend Christmas 2012 with his family rather than watching me unpack my coat).

It's alright, the guard said. You have a nice smile. I'll let you in.

That's sweet, I thought. But also moronic. It was sweet that he had complimented my smile and mentioned nothing of the fact that I am clearly some sort of woman-child (who carries a bouncy ball with them?). But moronic in the sense that, from the contents of my pockets, it is clear that I am not a stable human being.

Needless to say, I never again made the mistake of wearing my Parka coat to work.

PUSHING MY SUPERVISOR TO HIS ABSOLUTE LIMIT

I had been progressing really well. Feedback from direct observations from colleagues and managers had been great. I was feeling confident and needing less and less supervision. As a result my supervisor let me attend court without him. He tested me to make sure I knew what I was doing. I responded like a teenage girl, sighing at being patronised so much: *Jeez! Yes, I get it. I have done this before, remember.* Little did I realise that in four hours time I would have made a mistake so monumental that I convinced myself that when my supervisor saw me, he was probably going to have to kill me.

The key to this lesson is to never be scared to ask for help. Ever. No matter how much you think you should know something, if you have an inkling of doubt: ASK! I am screaming this lesson to myself as I type this in the hope that, somehow, I will be able to shout through space and time to stop me making the stupid mistake I made. Dear neighbours, I apologise.

It is clear that I need more information on this boy, the nightmare began. The judge glared down her nose at me through her half-moon glasses. *I require a Pre-Sentence Report from the Youth Justice Service.*

Pre-Sentence Report...PSR, I thought to myself. *That's easy. They take three ...weeks? Or is it days?* The other court officer had stepped out of court temporarily to deal with a crisis elsewhere. The correct thing to do would have been to confidently inform the terrifyingly imposing judge that I did not know how long it would take and would need to converse with my colleague. However, the judge's unshakeable glare and her obviously superior intellect made that prospect unbearably embarrassing.

It'll be ready in three days, I said, loudly and stupidly.

Fantastic, the judge responded. The ecstatic tone in her voice hit me in the chest like a cold knife. I realised immediately that a PSR takes three weeks not three days. Before I could rectify the situation the case had been closed and the courtroom cleared. I remember moving very slowly from then onwards. I was hoping that I would maybe never have to leave the courtroom and therefore never have to tell anyone what had just happened. Sometimes my brain does not think rationally.

Unfortunately, the distance from the courtroom to my office is a short one and so I eventually found myself back at my desk. Trying desperately not to cry or be sick with fear, I headed straight for Rachel.

Rachel was one of the senior officers on my team; she has a planet-sized brain and, luckily for me, the patience of a saint. Half of everything I know about Youth Justice I learned from Rachel on one of our many journeys to the local Young Offenders Institution. I would quiz her for hours on every aspect of criminal justice that I needed clarifying. There must have been many a journey where Rachel wanted to steer the car into a wall to stop me talking, but she never showed it. I knew that if anyone could sort out the awful, awful mess I had created, it would be Rachel.

At first Rachel thought I was joking. When she finally realised I wasn't, she laughed for a good minute. I was not in a place to laugh with her. My forehead rested firmly on the desk. *Well, first, you need to ring your supervisor*, Rachel told me. I rang Phil and got an incredibly calm and sweet response. I later found out that Rachel had pre-warned him that I wasn't taking the situation well.

The next three days would be hell on earth for me, Rachel and Phil. There were 8am starts, 9pm finishes and approximately 300 miles of driving to get all the necessary information from the right people. Rachel and Phil did the driving; without them I would have turned up to court empty-handed. Thanks to their help though, I managed to complete the report. The judge complimented my work, but by that time I was so exhausted I could barely hear. The incident of the 'three day PSR' will be etched in on my brain forever, along with the words *never be afraid to ask for help*.

STATUTORY BUREAUCRACY

Having now had experience of several different Youth Justice Services, and seeing and hearing about how different statutory services worked, I found myself bothered by one particular problem. Statutory settings seemed to be governed by what resources were available rather than what worked. As a social work student, the term 'evidence-based practice' had been routinely drilled into me, and yet seemed nowhere to be seen in reality. As a result, I ended up writing the following blog, critiquing the Youth Justice Board and what I believed to be the failings in the system. I must stress here that this is merely my opinion. When I first wrote this blog people made out that I was single-handedly trying to dismantle the entire Youth Justice system. If only I had that power.

Youth Justice will help you lose four stone in a week

I have been taking some herbal pills, called Acai berries, for four months. The Daily Mail dubbed these pills 'botox in a bottle' or 'youthberry' because of its amazing ability for weight loss. I religiously take three pills a day, and since doing so I have lost three stone. I feel so much better for it and am finally within my BMI. The anti-oxidants have cleansed my body and boosted my metabolism. Acai berries really do contribute to rapid weight loss.

Except, of course, they don't.

If I had been thinking rationally, I would have realised at the point of reading The Daily Mail review, that if they're championing Acai, then the pills definitely don't work. However, I seem to have convinced myself (and everyone in the office) that these pills DO work. My weight loss is nothing to do with the fact that my new job has created a lifestyle change where I can no longer eat all day, every day. Nor is it anything to do with the fact that my car has broken down and I have had to start walking everywhere. Nope. It's just the pills.

People know, deep-down, that diet pills don't work. It's a truth that no one wants to openly acknowledge. Like when you organise a BBQ in England and convince yourself that it won't rain that weekend. It's a lie we tell ourselves in order to fight off the miserable reality that is British weather and Asda microwave meals. I've convinced myself that diet pills work to fight off the reality that if I want to lose weight I have to go to the gym and be the fat, red, sweaty girl who sits between the woman who has the body of a super-model and apparently has an inability to sweat; and the gorgeous man who makes you go ten times redder than you already are. That's reality. And I don't like it.

The Youth Justice System is similar to diet pills. More specifically, the programmes that are put in place to deal with the most prolific and high-risk offenders in our community, are like diet pills.

One of the main aims of the Youth Justice Board is to prevent offending and reoffending by children and young people under the age of 18. Nationally, an Intensive Programme is offered to courts to say that offenders can be dealt with in the community rather than sent to prison. The Intensive Programme promises to: address the underlying causes of the offending; manage the risks posed by the young person to the community; stabilise what is often a very chaotic lifestyle; and help the young person lead an independent life free of offending (Youth Justice Board website).

Except of course, it doesn't.

Re-offending rates consistently remain around the 70 per cent mark. Nationally, the Youth Justice system is not successfully meeting the Youth Justice Board's main aim. It's almost as if evidence-based practice doesn't exist in the world of Youth Justice. But like diet pills, no one wants to openly admit it, because it would result in a lot of work.

There are two things that need to be noted: first, that those young people on Intensive Programmes are some of the most heavily entrenched offenders and come from extremely chaotic and damaging backgrounds; therefore there is no quick-fix. Second, the Youth Justice Board's aim is unrealistic. They will never prevent all offending. Crime is a social construct and will always exist. However, it is apparent through my work within the Youth Justice system that we aren't giving the most serious offenders the right support. We may never get rid of all crime, but we can surely reduce the re-offending rate from 70 per cent?!

High case loads, poor resources and lack of training mean that in reality a young person on an Intensive Programme is only seen briefly each day. The rest of the time the Youth Justice officer in charge will be ringing around schools and colleges ensuring the young person is attending education; completing risk assessments on paper; attending approximately five million social care meetings a month (accurate statistics); completing risk assessments on paper; liaising with the police, completing risk assessments on paper and typing up every conversation they've had with everyone. Oh, and typing up risk assessments on paper. While all these things are important, it leaves very little time to spend with the young person, never mind try and address offending behaviour in a meaningful manner.

Maybe things would be different if resources in the community hadn't been almost completely obliterated. Previously, if a young person was involved in gun crime, there was a charity providing a targeted gun crime programme that Youth Justice workers could send that young person to on a weekly basis. Now, however, less of these services exist, so Youth Justice workers are supposed to deliver that service; workers who have no knowledge or experience in educating young people on gun crime. If programmes existed in the community to provide meaningful intervention, where young people actually interacted positively with professionals over a number of hours a week, then maybe we would see some positive results. But group work programmes and relationship-based practice seem to be massively undervalued in social work at present, and these programmes simply don't exist.

For those quick-thinkers out there who are shouting – Well, why don't you just send them to prison then rather than try and manage them in the community? – prison is equally ineffective and arguably causes more problems in the long-run. The term 'University of Crime' is a depressingly fitting description of prison.

The answer is having more time to implement effective programmes. Much like losing weight; if you want to really implement change, you have to put some physical effort in. We need to spend time and energy with these young people to run challenging programmes that address issues such as conflict resolution and victim awareness. Research shows again and again that the most effective way to engage with young people and change attitudes is through face-to-face work and through the relationship they build with professionals. This is what the evidence shows, but instead the focus remains on paperwork, bureaucracy and RISK MANAGEMENT (tears hair out).

Many of the practitioners I have worked with in Youth Justice are the most passionate, hard-working people I know and are firmly committed to social justice. The changes to the system would only have to be small to impact greatly. Practitioners are begging for the change. The biggest hurdle is one common to social work in general; we need to acknowledge risk, but not shy away from it; acknowledge that mistakes do happen and that we don't always need to blame someone for it; and acknowledge that paperwork does not reduce risk.

There are no quick fixes in life. Acai pills included. So to all the ladies in the office who I have convinced to spend a small fortune on these pills, I apologise!

This blog comes with a health warning. After writing it, a lot of people I had previously worked with took offence at what I had said. Some people agreed with me; some people agreed with the essence of what I was saying but didn't think I should have said it publicly; others didn't agree with what I had said at all. Consequently, I got into quite a bit of trouble and was put in a very vulnerable position, job-wise. I lost friends and professional relationships as a result, and was incredibly upset and stressed about the situation.

Two years later, do I look back on the incident and wish I hadn't printed it? No. And for the simple reason that I stand by what I said and am entitled to my opinion. Of course, I never wanted to cause anyone offence and was incredibly upset at the reactions I got from people who I thought knew me better. This blog was only ever meant as a prompt for discussion around something that I *really* care about. Every statutory service I have worked for has been brilliant and I was not criticising a specific service but rather expressing my concerns about the welfare and criminal justice systems in place in this country.

Getting into trouble was a valuable lesson for me and really tested whether I was willing to put my neck on the line for what I believed to be right. I would advise anyone who puts their name to any public criticisms to be absolutely sure that they believe in what they are saying and are willing to take criticism back. There will always be people who disagree with what you think, but never be afraid to stand up for what you believe in. You may not be right, but as long as you do not cause harm to those you have a duty to protect, you are free to express yourself.

8 The fear

TWO YEARS' EXPERIENCE OR MORE

As the finish date of the social work Masters drew closer, there was a palpable sense among my cohort, of what can only be described as mania. Almost everyone I knew on my course seemed to have an intense fear of finishing. For some the fear was centred around getting a job. For others it was finalising the large amount of written assessments. For others it was a terrible combination of both, with the added stress of wondering whether they had chosen the right occupation. I fell into the last category and, true to form, I responded to the stress with hysteria and alcohol. My level of irrationality reached dizzying new heights.

On 17 December, 2011, I woke up with an earth-shattering headache and overwhelming sense of embarrassment. The previous evening had been the night of our course Christmas party. Rather than socialise and enjoy the company of my course mates and lecturers, I had decided a few weeks previous that there was not a single second of any day that should be wasted doing anything other than job hunting. I had convinced myself that if I didn't get a job in July then I would not be able to pay rent, which would mean I would end up back in Morecambe working in a chippy until I was 50 and my main motivation for getting up in the morning would be the prospect of a free chip bun after a 12-hour shift. This thought plagued me.

So there I was, at 11pm on a Friday night, as my friends intermittently sent me texts about how great their night out was, looking through job advert after job advert. Of course, most jobs required an immediate start, and as I didn't finish my course for another six months, I could not apply. By the time I reached my 500th application, which stated I must have *two years or more post qualifying experience*, something in my chip bun-obsessed head snapped. Within ten minutes I had put on the first dress I could find, dry shampooed my hair, hailed a taxi, and found myself at the bar with my friends having just ordered a round of tequilas. My last memory is being fireman-lifted out of a bar by a bouncer who clearly had not appreciated my need to dance past closing time.

Fortunately for me, my landlord, and my liver, I did find a job which I would start the day after my second placement finished. Applying early definitely paid off but it would be fair to say that, at times, job hunting got the better of me.

SOCIAL WORK LIFE CRISIS

What scared me most, however, was not the idea of living for chip buns, although I was having frequent nightmares about it. But this was nothing compared to the crippling sense of anxiety I felt when I asked myself the question, *have I chosen the right profession?* Towards the end of my second placement I wrote this blog on the internet, prompting concern about me from friends and colleagues, but most notably, the new man I was dating, who read it and quickly called his friend for a second opinion. After reading it my now-partner's friend advised him to steer well clear of me as I was clearly unhinged. I would have given the same advice to be fair:

 Social work life crisis

So… this weekend I told a 12-year-old girl she will never find happiness.

No, I'm not proud of myself but it happened, okay.

I was at a 50th birthday party and there was a free bar. A group of 12-year-old girls had been talking about boys all evening. In fact, they had been talking about boys longer than I had been drinking. Then one of them made the fatal mistake of asking my opinion on whether she should text a boy. (I would like to remind everyone at this point that I have recently come out of a long-term relationship, and, as I said before, the bar was free. FREE, people!)

My answer to the girl was something along the lines of:

Boys are exciting at your age. Relationships are exciting and hopeful. And that's good and nice (wine spilling out of my glass). But very quickly the Disney promise of a Prince Charming (hic!) will show itself as the cruel lie it is and love will become painful and problematic (hic!) But if you're lucky, and haven't messed up your future for some 16-year-old in a band, you will throw your hopes and dreams into a career. And you'll work hard towards that career goal, which you think will give you a sense of validation (hic!). But then one day something will happen to make you realise that even your hopes and dreams can let you down and life is ultimately meaningless. So in conclusion, girls (hic!), text them, don't text them, do what you want, because ultimately, you will never find happiness.

My favourite reaction to my shattering of a child's hopes, was from a colleague, who didn't disagree with my pessimistic outlook on life, or blatant bitterness. She just calmly replied: They're supposed to find that out for themselves you know.

I think it's safe to say I'm having a bit of a career crisis at the moment. At work people no longer bother asking me how I am for fear of the morbidity of the reply. I am not depressed. I'm just at a crossroads in my social work career, near graduation, where I have to decide if this is really the job for me. And I'm not sure it is. There are so many aspects of social work that I detest. Many things do not make sense to me and many more things that make me think that social work does more harm than good. Consequently, the last few weeks at work have involved me having a daily mini breakdown.

And it happens in all professions. My friend is the head of marketing for a large internet company and she recently had a breakdown of epic proportions. I'm not sure of all the details, but some of the texts I received from her over the following week included:

Everyone in the office is smiling at me a lot. I think they think I'll start crying again.

The warehouse boys are scared to put paperwork on my desk. They have brought me a cake instead. They'll be padding the walls next.

I'm sure everyone has bad weeks at work where they wonder if they've chosen the right career path. The problem with social work is that, for most social work students, it is a calling; a profession that encompasses everything you think, feel and believe; a way of life. So when you doubt that social work is the right job for you, you automatically fall into a spiral of questions culminating in who am I? *and* what is the point in life?

Of course the unexamined life is not worth living. But bloody hell, asking yourself what the point of me is every Monday morning when you're on your third chocolate digestive and half-way through ANOTHER risk assessment is a bit much.

Social work seems to have become a nine-to-five profession for many people. The professionalisation of the job has some obvious advantages, however the many disadvantages are becoming more and more apparent to me. Too often do I ring an agency for support with a young person in desperate need of help, only to be told that it's out of hours *and there's not a lot that can be done now. I went into this job to help people in need. Within social work, the help I can offer seems so constrained by risk management and bureaucracy, so that rather than actually help people, I spend most of my time filling in forms about them.*

A young boy I work with recently rang me at 7pm, hysterical and refusing to go home due to ongoing problems. He had rung me for help. But of course, for health and safety, and policy and procedure reasons, rather than drive to the boy to calm him down and return him home, I had to ring four different agencies to see if they could offer him some support for the night. It's not in my job description to help him in the evenings and, as a student, I would have been removed from placement if I'd gone to see him. So I spent the evening ringing agencies and filling in the relevant paperwork while a 14-year-old boy walked the streets in the pouring rain, in tremendous distress. No agencies were able to help him. He stayed out all night. I sat in my warm house, feeling utterly useless.

The next day my supervisors could see that I was annoyed about the situation. They tried to justify the actions we had to take by talking about empowerment, dependency, risk and not being a 'Rescuer', etc., etc. But none of that really sits well with me. I don't seem to buy into the social work 'doctrine'. And for that reason I'm not sure if I'm made to be a social worker.

There is a quote by Jan de Hartog that says: Do not commit the error, common among the young, of assuming that if you cannot save the whole of mankind you have failed. *I think an error, common among some of the more experienced social workers, is to think that just because we may not be able to save the whole of mankind, doesn't mean that we shouldn't give it a good go.*

Anyway, my brain is still fried and I will probably read this outpouring tomorrow to realise it is not in sentences. I'll let you know if I make it to graduation!

The boy I was referring to was Adam.

ALEX

I was not the only person on my course to feel the overwhelming weight of the power and responsibility we would soon possess. Alex, a student in the same year as me, is an incredibly bright and inspiring woman, and not one who I would expect to have struggled. I would always see her in the library, casually putting top class pieces of work together in a matter of hours. She writes here, quite openly about her experience of the course:

Bar maid to social worker

Social worker is a pretty natural career progression from bar maid, right? Well, that's what I argued at my course interview, waxing lyrical about transferable skills; working under pressure, remaining calm while negotiating (ok, arguing) with drunks, being committed to maintaining confidentiality (I know things about my former regulars that really did make my hair curl).

The University of Sheffield agreed and duly offered me a place. The course was a positive experience, but also a steep learning curve, since I had minimal knowledge of the vagaries of the UK social care system and little grounding in sociological theory. Nevertheless, I attacked the academic challenges enthusiastically; excelled in presentations and seminars, and scraped through the excruciating torture of the law exam.

My first placement was in a Women's Aid refuge (surrounded by other feminists – yes!), and I passed with flying colours. I also, however, began to worry. A lot. I mean, if you serve someone a bad pint, you upset someone's stomach, but if you make a bad decision as a social worker, you upset someone's life.

Dwelling on this weight of responsibility, I remained committed to helping people, but deeply questioned my ability to achieve this. I thought I would never know enough; felt I was 'soft' for being deeply moved by the horrors that my service users shared with me, and despaired at the ever-shrinking resources available to us in tackling the social issues we face (thanks, coalition government).

Things came to a head in my second year when, bogged down in personal troubles and panicking that I would never a social worker make, I realised that my second placement filled me not with excitement, but dread. I cried hysterically at my bemused course leader, who begged me not to quit (the best compliment I've ever had) and suggested a leave of absence. It was the best thing I ever did, and I realised that to get anywhere I had to stop trying to be superwoman, and accept my limitations.

On my final placement in a mental health team, something strange happened. Colleagues from other disciplines asked my advice and respected my opinion; service users appreciated that I was able to explain the system to them, and their families thanked me for my honesty and

*genuine concern. Student practice made me realise that I did have some-
thing to offer, and also that I had learned a tremendous amount without
really noticing.*

*I still worry about meeting the challenges of social work, but I now appre-
ciate the tools I have to tackle those challenges. The best advice I had
is that all you can offer social work is yourself, and learning to look after
myself if I'm to be any use at all was the most significant lesson. Social
work is the profession for me after all, because at heart it's about people,
just like being a bar maid.*

IDEALISM LOST

Young social workers are often told off for their desire to rescue and their idealism. This is
something that *really* pissed me off at the time, and still does. My experience is that people
who tell you to stop being idealistic are the ones who let the bad stuff get them down.

I have a great love for inspirational quotes. When I was younger I used to find as many
as I could on the internet and write out my favourites in my neatest writing. All four walls
of my room were covered from floor-to-ceiling with wise words from wise people. I have
kept up this habit, only now the quotes end up tattooed on my body rather than stuck up
on my wall. A few of the quotes that never fail to motivate me are:

> **Never doubt that a small group of thoughtful, committed, citizens can change
> the world. Indeed, it is the only thing that ever has.**
>
> **—Margaret Mead**

> **Always aim for the Moon, even if you miss, you'll land among the stars.**
>
> **—W. Clement Stone**

I could go on forever.

Throughout my two-year course, I met several practitioners who would sigh and roll their
eyes whenever I questioned the injustice of the criminal justice system. Why, for example,
do we continue to make the youth court system so impenetrably difficult to understand?
Many young people charged with a crime leave court with no clue of what has just happened. *That's just the way it is*, I would be told, as if we as practitioners have no power to
ask for change, never mind effect it. The best social workers are the people who I have
met who refuse to sacrifice what is right for what is easy. As I get older I haven't stopped
being idealistic. I just hide it better to avoid other people's negativity.

Being faced with bureaucracy and a lack of enthusiasm from professionals from various
organisations had a profound effect on me. The problem with being an idealist is you
always expect the best from everyone. And you expect better than the best from yourself.

While I will always hold the utmost respect for those who refuse to compromise what is right for what is easy, I now understand why some people settle for less. Life can get in the way, and frankly the stress can kill you.

STRESS

March of 2012 brought my first bout of serious stress-related illness. Having never been truly stressed before, I had no idea what was happening to me. Everything was getting on top of me and up until now I had spent 24 hours a day living and breathing social work. I would happily work 12-hour days and prioritise work over socialising. It must have been so obvious to more experienced practitioners what was going to happen to me.

It began subtly. Whenever I went out for lunch, it would take me forever to decide what to eat. I simply couldn't make a decision. It really didn't matter what I ate (I'm certainly not a fussy eater) but it was as if every lunch-time was a life-and-death decision. And then, when I finally got to the counter, I couldn't remember the pin number for my debit card. I began forgetting more and more simple things; my postcode, my phone number. Then, one day, I was in the toilets at work and I knocked my hand on the sink. Something inside me cracked. I burst into tears and slumped to the floor. I could not stop crying, not even to catch my breath. Everything was fine. Why was I crying? I didn't *feel* stressed.

Stress management was not discussed much at university. The one thing I wish they had drilled into us during training is the need to look out for each other as social workers. You simply cannot be a social worker if you don't practice good self-care. There are no exceptions to this rule.

Other people on my course had integrated coping mechanisms into their lives. Some exercised, some meditated, some drank. The ones who managed stress most success-fully were those who had a space in their life which was purposefully separate from social work. They had several hours in each day where their focus would not, and could not, be on work; it was a time to recover from the day's challenges.

The fact is, even when you know better, everyone thinks they can tell when someone will or won't struggle. People can hold it together but be like ducks, paddling frantically away beneath the water. An accumulation of stress can lead to depressive illness.

Dr Timothy Cantopher describes depressive illness as *the affliction of the good and the great* and names Abraham Lincoln, Vincent Van Gogh and Ernest Hemingway as some of the many who have suffered with it. It is ESSENTIAL – I cannot stress this enough – for the future of social work, that we are open about our limitations.

SPIRITUALITY

So what saved me from this pit of despair I was in?

It's very simple: excellent supervision. The first person who saved me from my spiral of self-loathing, self-doubt and stress was Kima, my personal tutor at the University of Sheffield. Kima is to me what Yoda was to Luke Skywalker. Her only fault being that she never taught me how to master a light-sabre. Everything she said was a pearl of wisdom and so intelligent that the full meaning would not truly resonate with me until weeks later. I enjoyed visiting Kima's office. It reminded me of a fortune teller's cave. The room was dark, filled with a strangely reassuring smell of smoke, and you knew upon entering that you would leave with a greater understanding of your place within the social work profession.

Kima never said what you wanted to hear, but rather told you what you needed to hear. She pulled no punches. Whenever I thought I had really mastered a theory or a type of intervention, I would speak to Kima and feel that I knew less than ever before. And it is essential that you have someone who challenges every aspect of your practise as there are no right answers in social work. Kima reminded me that every decision I make is based in a context of who I am, my past experiences, my recent reading, my recent experiences, and my values. Analysing who I was, what things I valued, and why I valued them, helped me make sense of myself as a social worker.

Discussions with Kima could go on for hours, without me noticing. Both Louise and I said that after we'd seen Kima we felt refreshed, as if our brains had had a three-hour massage. Upon completion of our Masters, Louise and I got celebratory tattoos (sorry, Mum). I have no doubt that Kima was one of the factors that led to Louise getting the tattoo: *Wise is she who knows she does not know.* Kima will always be, for me, one of those people who inspire you to know more.

The other person central to my recovery was my placement supervisor, Declan. While I had known Declan for years, our interactions had always been brief and infrequent. As my placement supervisor I would see Declan every two weeks for several hours. Within three meetings I became fully convinced that I had found in Declan a soul mate.

I'm not entirely sure of the official definition of a soul mate, nor even if there is such a thing, so let me explain. Declan understood me completely. And not the public, jokey, confident me, but rather every aspect that went into making *me*. He knew what made me sad and knew what needed to be resolved in order to make me a better practitioner.

I enjoyed Declan's company like I hadn't enjoyed anyone's company for a while. Due to him being male, and me female, I have no doubt people gossiped. But the beauty of my relationship with Declan was that it was not complicated by romantic feelings. It was, and still is, a friendship in the purest form I have ever experienced.

I connected with Declan on a spiritual level. I have an unshakeable belief that there is another plane to my existence. It's difficult to explain the feeling. For those who aren't spiritual, I guess one analogy would be the feeling music can invoke in people. It doesn't matter whether I'm on a bus or lying on my bed, when I listen to Tracy Chapman I am always somewhere else. My spiritual plane is as important, if not more important, than the physical one, and it is essential that I nourish it to keep myself happy and healthy. A year after qualifying, I have realised that I succumb most easily to stress when I am neglecting my spirituality.

I am not suggesting that being spiritual is an essential quality of being a social worker. Not at all. What I am saying is that you need to find what makes you, you, and make sure that you care for that aspect. Declan recognised this aspect of me.

He recommended books to me that changed my life and continue to help me when I am struggling. *The Prophet* by Khalil Gibran is one of those books. He also taught me the following proverb which is an excellent lesson to keep in mind for managing stress. I'll let you ponder it yourself:

A samurai master wanted to test his three sons to see what they had learned from his teachings. He placed a cushion above the door to his office and summoned his first son in.

The first son entered the office, and not noticing the cushion, it fell on his head.

The son had failed.

The samurai master re-positioned the cushion above the door and called in his second son.

The second son entered the room and sensing the falling cushion, rapidly drew his sword and sliced the cushion in two so it could not fall on him.

The son looked for approval from his father, but he too had failed.

The samurai master re-positioned the cushion and called the third son.

The third son approached but had noticed the cushion above the door and so, before entering, he carefully removed it and placed it on the floor.

The son had pleased his father for he had noticed the cushion above the door.

Keith

Spirituality and religion are aspects of social work that are rarely discussed. I find that odd, considering there is no greater support than if you are able to draw on the internal and external strength that spirituality can bring. Keith is a social worker who has been practising for many years. Here he talks about the importance of his faith to his profession:

Things are very different to what they were when I left school in the mid-1970's. Fewer people than today went on to further study. The expectations of lads like me from the local housing estate were not very high. With four O-levels I had no trouble finding employment.

As I got older I began to think about concepts like job satisfaction, and about what I was doing and how I was contributing to society. Although I was not aware of the term 'value base' I knew that there was something that made me tick, something that helped me make sense of the world and who I was. It became clear that I was not happy or fulfilled in my job. I had a conversation with a friend and something she said changed everything: Why don't you try one of the caring professions?

To me this meant being a nurse. You need to understand that a young lad from a housing estate in Stenhousemuir should not be thinking about being a nurse – that's for girls! In the end, I signed up for CSV – Community Service Volunteers – and agreed to accept their first offer of a voluntary position. It was at a hostel for young offenders in Northampton that I began my career in social care. I worked in the voluntary sector for 11 years before going on to becoming a qualified social worker. I consider myself to be a man of faith. It's this that helps me make sense of things.

There is no doubt that social work is a worthy profession. There are resonances between people of faith and social work. Not that you have to be a person of faith to be a good social worker. But remember these are personal reflections.

Social work is a stressful career. However, in among the anxiety, the managerialism, the paperwork, the cuts and the bureaucracy, there are things and people that surpass all these.

Social workers are primarily people who serve. If you keep this to the forefront of your mind you will be able to cope with some of the negative things mentioned above. Also at the forefront of your mind should be the human worth of all the people who use social care services. An area of work that has given me particular pleasure has been teaching others as a practice educator and for nine years as an associate lecturer with the Open University.

Difficulties in social work will always be there, but there are things that you can do that will help you keep your focus on service. Join BASW and take an active part in your profession. Join another group that reflects who you are. In my case it's Social Work Christian Fellowship. Read about the history of social work and the work of the early pioneers who are not with us now.

Finally, if I can mention an unsung hero who has made a huge contribution to social work: Bob Holman. Check him out, read his writings and enjoy your career making a difference and serving others.
—Keith Malcolm, currently on secondment in a Shared Lives Team in Derbyshire, writing in a personal capacity.

ANTI-OPPRESSIVE BINGO

I recently attended some incredible training on Understanding Abuse Linked to Witchcraft, Juju and Spirit Possession presented by Leethen Bartholemew and Gary Foxcroft from The Witchcraft and Human Rights Information Network (WHRIN). If you ever get the chance to attend, grab the opportunity with both hands. A few months ago my friend pointed out to me that there was a multitude of orange vans driving around Sheffield; I went from never noticing them to seeing approximately three a day. In much the same way, after attending the WHRIN training I realised that I have never noticed witchcraft and spirit-based abuse, not because it didn't exist but because I wasn't looking for it. Victoria Climbié and Kristy Bamu are just two cases which demonstrate how real an issue it is in Britain. After the training I began thinking back to cases I had worked where I suspect I may have missed the religious aspect to their problems.

As social workers it is essential that we are culturally sensitive. One of the key assessments during my Masters course was filling in the Anti-Oppressive Grid, which tested your ability to identify power imbalances in your practice. The grid covered race, class, gender, disability and religion. I really resented the grid format we were given. It felt almost as if we were playing bingo with our case load, ensuring that we worked with at least one person, different from ourselves, from each category. But my gripes aside, it really is imperative that we are able to identify the subtle influences of people's social make-up. Faith, particularly, is absolutely central to the way people live their lives. Practices that may be viewed as abusive by many Europeans are normal in other religious communities. Fasting, for example, is a problem that commonly causes young Muslim people to leave home. They may not want to engage in Ramadan but their parents will not provide them with food as they are worried what will happen if their child does not observe Islam. The parents are not acting out of malice but rather from a desire to save their child's soul. Social workers need to recognise the immense power of faith. Religious belief is not something that can be counselled away. We can see this from the large number of homosexual people who sadly take their own lives due to disapproval, not only from their religious communities, but from an internalised sense of being evil.

Talking about spirituality in Britain is difficult. We live in a largely secular society which takes spirituality about as seriously as superstition. Whether it be the social worker utilising it for self-care, or accepting it as a major force in a service user's life, spirituality and faith cannot be ignored. For me, a major shift in focus is needed in this area for the future success of our profession.

So are you a social worker or not?

OH, I THOUGHT YOU'D BE DOING SOMETHING BETTER THAN THIS!

Despite being at the coal-face of social problems, my experience is that social workers in the voluntary sector are often looked down upon. On finding out that my new job would be at a homeless charity I received lovely comments from former course mates such as: *Ooh, I never thought you'd be in the voluntary sector. I always thought you'd be doing something bigger!* Talk about a back-handed compliment. It rivals the time my doctor placed me on the weighing scales and responded with a surprised: *Don't you hold all that weight well?*

The key to me being the first person on my course to get a job was the fact that I was willing to look at the voluntary sector. While I was sure that I still wanted to be a social worker, I knew that the answer to my survival would be to avoid rigid and bureaucratic practice. I needed the freedom of the voluntary sector. A job had come up in the city I was living in which combined my two Masters placements perfectly; I would be working with homeless young people who were involved with the Youth Justice system.

During my interview I asked whether I would be able to undertake the Assessed and Supported Year in Employment, which was an integral part of my development as a NQSW. When the interview panel said yes, I knew that this job was pretty close to perfect for me. Others from my course held out for a statutory role. While they all ended up in jobs, they did have to spend several months living with their parents, claiming benefits. That was not an option for me.

It became clear to me very early on that the voluntary sector, while it avoided the stresses of too much paperwork, created different stresses of its own. Eighty per cent of my week is spent with my service users, which is exactly what social work practice should be like. However, the range of problems you have to deal with can become quite overwhelming. There was one week in which I had to deal with a rape, a gang shooting, a drugs den and a group of sex offenders who had created a squat in one of our properties. Of course, not every week is like that, but as we are the professionals that service users see the most, we are often the ones who receive upsetting disclosures or stumble across weapons stashed in our properties. It is high-risk work, both physically and emotionally, but in a way that is what makes it all the more worthwhile.

CARLOS

Carlos qualified in the same year as me from the University of York. I met Carlos at a BASW conference and was intrigued by the path he had taken since graduating. Here he blogs about why he avoided the statutory sector:

Be flexible

So where am I now?

Unemployed.

Only joking, although when I qualified I did spend a few months unemployed and on benefits, that's what benefits are for, to help people out in times of trouble. After almost a year since qualifying, I am working six jobs across children's and families, local authority and voluntary sectors.

Why?

Because I love the diversity, I love working with people of all ages and backgrounds and in all situations, that's social work right? I need to spend 80 per cent of my time in the community, supporting people face to face (true social work in my opinion).

What's next?

Well, I have registered with some social work agencies but a few of them have come back saying that I need at least 12 months post-qualifying experience in a statutory setting. Boring! Talk about following the status quo and not wanting to rock the boat. There's no flexibility or creativity in that mentality at all. I would like to move into mental health and will be going back to university to do some short courses in counselling, something I wish had been covered more within the social work degree.

I may get stumped with social work as a job title in the future as I'm interested in therapeutic based social work. I don't mind, I'm a qualified social worker and I don't need a job title telling me that I am. What I do know is that I'm interested in working in this area. social worker is one of many job titles in this area; be flexible people.

I WISH YOU WAS MY SOCIAL WORKER

You ain't a social worker, Dale informed me very firmly. Dale was one of my first service users at my new job. He was an incredibly intelligent young man and had known me for four years when he made this remark.

I am, I contested.

Why you working in housing then? he responded, thinking he'd caught me out.

Because social workers can work in housing too, I retorted.

After a few seconds of squinting and contemplating my response, Dale said: *I wish you was my social worker.*

Well, if you think about it, I am your social worker, Dale, I said, trying to hide my frustration.

Nah. You ain't a social worker. Dale had made up his mind.

Dale summed up what most of the young people I work with think. Social workers are those people who work in Child Protection and Leaving Care. Sometimes they work in mental health, but mainly with families who are struggling.

I may not be able to convince the young people I work with that I am qualified, but one of the main benefits of being a social worker in a non-social work role is that you are able to advocate brilliantly for your service users. When I attend meetings with social services I have an in-depth knowledge of what service my service users are entitled to, and the resource limitations that may stop a young person getting what they want.

There was one incident where Dixie, a short-haired, feisty Geordie girl, could not understand why social services had come to her house to check on her little brother. Dixie was 16 and had been left to care for her five-year-old brother most nights while their mother went to the pub. I was able to explain to a very angry Dixie that social services weren't accusing her of being a bad sister but were worried about the responsibility that had been put on her. Dixie cried a lot during our conversation but was able to ask all the questions she needed answering about the social work system and what assessments might be carried out. She wasn't happy with the situation, but feeling armed with knowledge, she could accept what was happening and knew how she could take some control of it.

THE LONELY SOCIAL WORKER

I don't wear make-up. I mean, I probably should, but I am not a fan. Part of me feels like it is an essential part of my journey into womanhood, being able to master the art of make-up application. And I have tried, believe me. Several times I have asked a member of staff from Boots to explain to me the difference between concealer and foundation. They show me which brushes to use and in what direction to apply it. Obediently I buy the recommended products, take them home, and fail spectacularly to repeat what I have just been shown. My end product is always reminiscent of a sweaty and sad French mime artist.

Somewhat predictably then, when I am in a group of women who are talking about make-up, I feel very left out. I get the same feeling of isolation as being the only social worker in my non-social work team. While we do the same job, I am aware that I am not quite the same.

While most of my non-social work colleagues bring their own expertise and appreciate my unique contribution to the team, there are others who will happily tell me to leave my fancy theory at home as they're too busy working to have time to reflect. And you do begin to feel a bit cheeky if you spend an hour or two of your week just reading theory while others are busily attending keywork sessions. I have to firmly remind myself that practice without reflection is dangerous and I am not 'just reading'.

So how do you maintain a social work identity in a non-social work team? I am incredibly lucky that I was provided with access to a Practice Learning Consortium (PLC) run by a woman called Nell. Like most things, this service is soon to be cut due to funding issues, but I honestly would not have made a tenth of the progress I have made in my first year as a social worker if it weren't for the PLC.

Nell correctly said to me: *I think we need to understand clearly and be able to explain that we are social workers, whatever our job title, because of a particular combination of factors: our training, our qualification, our theory base, our methods, our values and our professional registration.* Social workers need to be proud of what they do and should not be afraid to use their skills in myriad roles.

SOCIAL WORK GUILT

Describing a day in the life of a social worker would be a pointless task. My day is completely different to those of my colleagues, and a world away from a social worker in a different service. Each day is unpredictable and often shaped by crises.

There are three things I have noticed to be fairly common among most social workers. These are:

1. *Taking pleasure in the smallest things*: Things we may often take for granted, such as someone turning up to meet you when you've made an appointment with them, can become major causes for celebration as a social worker. I almost held a Rio de Janeiro style carnival in the office the day I managed to support a young man into attending a Child Protection conference involving his child. Until that point, he had no concept that his child was at genuine risk of being taken from him.

2. *Risk radar always on high*: I am a nightmare to go on a night out with. My partner is convinced I have a sixth sense. Whenever I am sitting in a pub, I am able to tell you what is happening on every other table in the room. I know which couple are arguing, I know who's secretly taking drugs in the toilet, and I can predict with pin-point accuracy when a fight is about to break out. I do all this while fully engaging in conversation with the people I am with. Spending seven or eight hours a day working with people and trying to figure them out has given me this weird ability. It also means I will refuse to go in certain pubs and get on certain buses if I think I can sense trouble. As a social worker you will begin to notice social interactions that others won't.

3. *Social work guilt*: Another factor that makes me an unbridled joy to be with on nights out is my ever-present sense of guilt. I love champagne. It is one of my favourite treats, but I cannot truly enjoy it anymore knowing that one bottle is the equivalent of a full week's benefits for my service users. As a social worker based in a homeless charity, the strongest pangs of guilt I feel are when I see someone sitting at the side of the street without a home. The following blog sums up just some of the grief I impose on my friends when we go out drinking:

 # Money for the poor

I have this same debate at least once a month. Whenever I go for a night out in town, at some point I will always end up giving money to a homeless person. I have one friend whose obsession with dogs is bordering on unhealthy and so if I am with her at the time, I will sit and talk to the homeless person while my friend contemplates how she can smuggle their dog into her handbag without anyone noticing.

If I am with other friends, however, an argument will usually follow about how I shouldn't give money to those sort or people.

First, I am never sure what anyone means when they say those sort of people. You just mean people, right? Because I am pretty sure (although I spent the majority of GCSE biology writing quotes from The Office *on my textbook) we all share a similar biological make-up. Yes, some people dress different, have different cultures, a different way of life or even different coloured skin, but you can't separate us into 'sorts'. Some people seem to take great pleasure in categorising other people into groups that are 'lower' than themselves.*

My main problem, however, is why I shouldn't give a homeless person money. The common argument is, of course: They'll just spend it on drink or drugs.

That's nice. Usually, if I am on a night out in town, the contents of my purse is going on Wetherspoon's finest pint of Carling. So why shouldn't I allow someone else to make the same poor choice I'm making? When people refuse to give a homeless person money because they'll only spend it on drugs, *a voice in my head screams* what do you want them to spend it on? A three-piece suite? A kitchen cabinet? A chandelier for THE HOUSE THEY DON'T SODDING OWN?!

The response is always: You're making the problem worse.

I can categorically guarantee that I am not. I would never, ever advocate that someone use drink or drugs as a coping mechanism. When I give a homeless person, who is begging for money, twenty quid, it is so that they can spend it on food and shelter and whatever it is they need to keep them safe for another night. If that person chooses to spend that money on alcohol or drugs then that is their choice.

It is not for me to tell them how to spend it. Just like it's not for that person to tell me not to buy my fifth pint of Carling. We all make poor choices. I don't have a right to tell other people how to live because I have more money than them. I am not their superior, nor have I experienced their life. It is a sad reality that sometimes, drinking to forget will be the only way to make it to the next morning.

Additionally, I spend eight hours a day working to prevent homelessness and support homeless young people. I am not throwing money at a situation that is infinitely more complex than a lack of money. On a cold, rainy night, however, a twenty pound note may make a little difference.

There is a sense of superiority that people feel they have over those poorer than themselves. To decide whether what you are doing is right, ask yourself would you want to be told how to spend money that had been given as a gift? If it's a no for you, then it should be a no for all people.

So what have I learned? Advice for new social work students

The two-year course challenged me academically, practically and emotionally, and graduating is undoubtedly my proudest achievement to date. With that in mind, I have written down the key pieces of advice that I hope will make the course as enjoyable as possible for any new social work students embarking on this exciting journey:

Networking

If you have gained a place on a social work course, you will already have some relevant experience. Your course mates will have their own experience. Talk to as many people as possible. Tell them what you know and ask them what they know. In my first week, I spoke to a woman from my course who had volunteered to work with girls who had been sexually exploited. I had no knowledge of sexual exploitation when I began, but after a year I was writing my dissertation on *Relationship-based Practice and Sexual Exploitation*. Additionally, when I was on my first placement, I had a service user who was being sexually exploited and I knew which course mate to ask for advice about local resources. Speaking to others will open up numerous opportunities for you.

Read, read, read

Reading the basic legislation (Children's Act 1989, Mental Health Act 1983, Mental Capacity Act 2005, etc.) is an absolute must. However, you shouldn't stop there. Sign up to journals, read newspapers, keep up with developments online. My partner finds it very disconcerting that my room is filled with hundreds of articles on gang violence, but the more you read, the more knowledge you have to inform your practice!

Placement may not be perfect

Competition for placements is high, so try not to set your heart on one particular placement. Be as flexible as possible and if you get a placement in an area you really did not want, then take as much learning from that as possible.

What was it about the placement you did not like? What does that tell you about yourself? What would you like to gain from your next placement?

Peer supervision

My top tip is to find a friend from your course who you can discuss the challenges and successes of your day with (preferably over a glass of wine or two!). My course mate and I used to meet three times a week to listen to each other moan, and critique and praise the various aspects of our placements. We discussed policy and debated procedure and could do so with complete honesty. Sometimes you may not feel able to tell your placement supervisor all your deepest thoughts and fears, so having a friend who can support you is invaluable.

Social Media

I have become so addicted to Twitter that I have started using the term *hashtag* in everyday conversation. It's an incredibly irritating quality of mine, but is not worth sacrificing Twitter for. Having a Twitter account will give you access to social workers from all around the world. You will have easy access to a plethora of charities, jobs, papers and opinions. Just remember that whatever you write on the internet is accessible to anyone, so keep confidentiality.

Make the most of it

University will give you access to so much training, lectures, seminars and workshops. And they're all free extras. This doesn't last forever (trust me) and seminars can be expensive. Volunteer whenever you have spare time to gain more relevant skills.

Your social work course will hopefully only be the start of a long social work career. It is a challenging and sometimes disheartening profession which requires a lot of improvement, so BE KIND TO YOURSELF. Make sure you take time off when you need it and be honest with yourself about your limitations. Try not to let the bad aspects put you off, because I honestly believe that on a good day, social work is the best job in the world.

10 The Assessed and Supported Year in Employment

ASYE

So the day had finally come. I was a social worker. Did I feel different? Definitely. But that was mainly due to the gastroenteritis I managed to acquire on my second day of work, leading to me having to take time off in my first week. Other than the intense stomach ache, I felt the same. The transition from placement to real-world job had been seamless. I finished placement on the Friday and started work on the Monday; a factor which definitely meant I maintained my confidence. Several of my friends who did not find a job until months later talked of the anxiety they had at the thought of going back into practice. It had only been a few months but they were worried they had lost their knowledge and skills. Of course, none of them had.

I began the Assessed and Supported Year in Employment (ASYE) three months after I had started my job. This made it very hard when the ASYE supervisor came in and dictated what my work load should look like, how much study leave I should have, and my level of responsibility. It was clear from the outset that we would have to back-track a lot. Three months in, I already had an extremely hectic schedule. If the ASYE year had started the day I had started, it would not have been so fraught with tensions between myself, my managers and my ASYE supervisor as we negotiated what my work schedule should look like, but it certainly was a case of better late than never. Being an NQSW is more responsibility, means holding more cases, and is much more challenging. Having protective factors such as more supervision and a smaller case load put in place, gave me a sense of support and reassurance. I did not feel like I had been abandoned in the big, scary world of social work.

The assessed aspect of my Masters had been the driving force on both placements. The ASYE was different as it was very much in the background of my day-to-day work. In my experience, the emphasis has definitely been on the support aspect rather than the assessed aspect; and I have needed a lot of support over the last year.

MAYBE THERE HAS TO BE MORE TO LIFE THAN SOCIAL WORK

Three months into my ASYE, my mother was diagnosed with cancer. For anyone who's not experienced the threat of losing a parent, I can safely tell you that there are few things in life which have the power to knock you completely off balance. It doesn't matter how strong you are, or how well you have coped before; in fact, the stronger you are, the harder you fall.

Luckily, my mother was given the all-clear in March 2013 and is back to her lovely, bouncy self. The threat of losing her, however, has stayed with me and drastically changed my outlook on life. I had to spend several weeks caring for her when she was in hospital. Initially, I refused to take time off. Actually, I totally refused to acknowledge the fact that I wasn't sleeping, eating, or smiling very much anymore. I really did not want to be viewed as 'weak', especially as a newly qualified social worker desperately trying to prove herself.

During the time Mum was in hospital, I was reading Jeanette Winterson's *Why Be Happy When You Could Be Normal?* (I also read Sylvia Plath's *The Bell Jar* in the same week. One of the best pieces of advice I can give to anyone is to *not* read either of these books if you are feeling down. They are not feel-good reads, believe me). There is a quote in Jeanette's book which reads: *Anything outside of you can be taken away at any time. Only what is inside you is safe.* I cried when I read this line. I wanted to find some peace or some meaning that I could take from this and transform my unhappiness. But I just ended up thinking, *not even the inside is safe.* You can change at any moment; have an accident, take the wrong drug, wake up hearing voices, die. Or, you could have been so badly damaged by someone else that you do not know how to control how you feel or how you behave. Your inside is not in your control, nor is it safe. Ultimately, nothing is safe.

Of course, my knowledge of 'the inside' not being safe had come from my work with service users. I realised that spending most of my time working with people suffering from incredibly sad circumstances had given me a very specific view of the world – and largely it was a negative one. My colleague recently said to me that she found herself staring at a group of children on the bus who were laughing and joking with each other in a well-behaved way. They were genuinely happy and causing no problems for anyone else on the bus. It grabbed her attention, because she had forgotten that teenagers could be like that. While no one is problem-free, it is easy to forget that not everyone experiences as immense suffering as the people who are in need of our services. As my Mum always says, we need to remind ourselves of the beauty in this world.

And there came the turning point for me. I realised that if my entire life is consumed by social work, then my view of the world will become very warped. The consequences of that are serious. I cannot simply pretend to ignore the fact that my job significantly impacts upon my perceptions, my values and my emotional health. It has to. If it didn't affect me then I would have no empathy skills and wouldn't be suitable for the job. If I ignore the negative impact that stories of abuse or neglect have on me, then I am doing both myself and my service users a disservice. I have to allow myself to be sad. If I don't, the stories I hear will eat me up in other ways. I will ultimately have a more negative view of the world, which will mean I am less able to maintain optimism and belief in the capacity for my service users to have positive outcomes.

When my Mum became ill, things at home had become very negative for me. The only way to counteract that negativity was by taking some time off work to find the beauty in this world. It wasn't easy for me to take time off; but it was 100 per cent the right thing to do.

IT'S NEVER A SIMPLE CASE OF WIN OR LOSE

My year was filled with numerous fascinating and exciting young people. I had an evening shift supporting a violent 16-year-old offender who had a fearsome reputation. I remember watching him fall asleep on the sofa wearing the new shoes Youth Justice had bought him for his catering college course – because they were the nicest shoes he had ever owned and he did not want to take them off. Seeing him curled up in a chair with his dressing gown on, he looked, for the first time, like a child. It is all too easy to forget that even the 'toughest criminals' I work with are only children.

Dale (the young man who decided on my behalf that I was not in fact a social worker) has been a recurring fixture throughout my social work journey. Aged 14 he was one of the young men on the arts course for young offenders that I had first volunteered with. During my voluntary placement, I frequently found him illegally squatting at my service users' houses. On my second placement I visited him in prison several times in preparation for his re-release into the community. When, in the first few months of my job, I received a referral for Dale, who was in need of housing, I was more than happy to be his worker. Dale is an incredibly likeable young man with an addictive personality. Don't get me wrong, most sessions would start with him screaming at me because he wanted something like a bus pass or a bigger TV than the one he had been provided with, but that's only because he didn't know how to express himself any other way. Dale carried with him a lot of anger and frustration. Given the right circumstances I have no doubt that Dale could have been a very successful lawyer. His ability to retain legal information is parallel to any lawyer I have met. Matched with his persistence, I'm sure he could make a persuasive case. So, while he shouted, it was never *at* me but rather near me. And whenever he shouted during a keywork session, he would always make sure he apologised profusely before he left, and routinely tell me *you're still the best worker, you know*. He was the definition of a charmer.

Having known Dale for four years meant he trusted me. Not completely, but enough to come to me in a crisis, which is more than he would do with many other workers. Like most young people who offend, he had grown up around unreliable and often deceitful adults. You don't know hard work until you have to work for a young offender's trust; it is a hard fight. But having that strong, open and honest, professional relationship with Dale enabled us to get a lot of good work done. I moved him into his flat and we established what he wanted to achieve. He wanted his own place. Over the next few months we worked to ensure he could manage the property, cook for himself, pay his rent, sort his bills and manage his visitors. There was the occasional argument, such as when Dale insisted he was going to set the 7ft pile of old furniture outside his flat on fire and have a bonfire. We had a little disagreement on that one. But ultimately Dale was ready and able to move on to his own place. I was and still am very proud of him.

Unfortunately, a few weeks before we could have applied for a flat for Dale, three of his friends were released from prison. Within two days Dale was back in court after several months of stability. As with most things in social work, it's never the case of it being a simple success. You can make a lot of important progress but it won't be the end of the story. It was the third time I'd seen Dale sent to prison. I'm not ashamed to admit that this time I cried when I saw the judge send him down.

Dale was recently released and came straight to the office to see me. I was out on a home visit, but he asked my manager if he could live with our service again, and whether I could be his worker. It gives me a really warm feeling knowing this. I will always hold hope that Dale will repay the harm he has done and make a success of his life.

FEELING LIKE A FRAUD

My father has a bizarre tendency to look at Google Maps before going on holiday. That way, when he arrives on a Greek island that he has never been to before, he can act like a psychic by knowing what is around each corner. It was impressive the first time he did it, when I did not know how he'd done it. Now, by the 300th time, it's not so impressive.

That sense of being a fraud is the same feeling I get when social work students ask me for advice on something. My current team accepts a lot of students for their first placement, which means I often have students shadowing me at work. They seem amazed when I can offer a solution to a problem they have, but in my head I feel like telling them it's because I've done something like this before. But that's the point of social work. The more experience you have, the more solutions you can apply to new situations. While you should always treat every case individually, the lessons you learned on placement will stay with you and make you feel more confident as a practitioner. I, for example, will always know to have information translated rather than interpreted when working with someone who does not speak English.

I could feel myself growing in confidence on a daily basis and felt able to handle anything that was thrown at me. All the theory and practice from my two-year course was beginning to crystallise with every new positive achievement from a service user. The incredible thing about social work, however, is that every person you meet is completely new and different, and you can never have the answers ready for everything.

SHELLY

It had been a quiet morning, but by lunch time one of my service users was staring into my CEO's eyes and screaming, *WHEN I SHOOT MYSELF, THAT WILL BE YOUR FAULT.* They'd never met each other before. Aside from all the million other things going through my head at the time, I remember thinking that my CEO must think I'm doing an absolutely brilliant job supporting young people if they are so unhappy with the service that they can scream things like that into his face. *Cheers Shelly*, I remember thinking, *as well as making me extremely worried about your mental health, you've probably lost me my job*. Thankfully, after the incident was over, my CEO saw me in the corridor and said thanks. I took this to mean that he was grateful that I had handled the situation so well, rather than being a sarcastic *thanks for ruining my organisation*. It definitely wasn't sarcastic. Definitely. I think.

Shelly had, without a doubt, the most upsetting and traumatic history I have ever heard. She was born into drug misuse and violence. She had been sexually, physically and emotionally abused since she was a baby, and had witnessed both parents attempt to kill each other. She watched her parents go to prison and was placed in care. What I learned about her past will haunt me forever, but more significantly, it will forever haunt her and make it incredibly difficult for her to lead a normal life.

Shelly had been working with me for six months when the above outburst happened. She had just turned 17 and was dressed from head to toe in diamante. Some of the outfits she used to turn up to the office in would have put Vivienne Westwood to shame. The girl had a unique style. Up until her outburst, Shelly had been making turbulent progress. While she had progressed into independent accommodation, which is what she wanted, and had built up a strong relationship with her social worker, support worker and myself, which meant she would access other forms of support, it was still proving very difficult to keep her safe from sexually exploitative men.

Something was clearly wrong for her to have had an outburst like the one I described. While she always struggled to regulate her behaviour, she had never been openly threatening to staff. It wasn't until two weeks later that Shelly disclosed to me that she had been badly beaten by her 'boyfriend' the day before the outburst, and had been given a cocktail of drugs by him over the weekend. Throughout the eight months I worked with Shelly I found that her reality seeped out. She was never able to tell professionals what was happening to her straight away. It was too traumatic for her, and she needed time to process it. You could always tell, however, by her mood, that something awful had happened.

Keeping Shelly safe was my priority. One of the main problems was that Shelly could not keep herself safe. When consistent and steady boundaries were implemented, such as placing her in 24-hour residential support, she responded by going missing for weeks on end and falling into the hands of men who were trafficking young women around the country. When we gave her the freedom she wanted, placing her in semi-supported accommodation and allowing her to decide her own visitors, she continually invited everyone she met to her property. Having the power to create her own boundaries led to Shelly having the outburst. She couldn't cope. But when moved back into more supported accommodation, she ran away again. I was at a loss.

Shelly would have outbursts of anger and make extreme demands. Sometimes these demands were met. Sometimes they weren't. Every time, her reaction was the same; she was not happy and would burst into tears. It was clear that it was not the demands she wanted meeting, but rather something to blame for her unshakeable sense of unhappiness. When she demanded more clothes from social services, the fact that she had to wear old clothes was the source of all her pain. But when the new clothes were bought, she would be reminded that the clothes weren't to blame. A few days later she would think of something else to focus on.

Shelly would, however, have moments of such clarity. She knew that her neglectful mother and abusive step-father had contributed to her emotional and mental instability and yet, as humans are wont to do, she still craved a relationship with both of them; if she blamed them too much, she wouldn't be able to have the relationship she so desperately wanted.

Shelly was a kind and loving person. She was fiercely loyal to anyone who she viewed as her friend, but as she often made friends with someone after one meeting, she was vulnerable to abuse and disappointment. When I took time off to look after my Mum, she found out why I was off and sent me the loveliest text promising me that she would *hold it down* till I got back, and try not to make unreasonable demands of my co-workers. She did indeed *hold it down*. I still have a photo of Shelly next to my desk from the day she cooked lunch for all the staff at my organisation. She had spent the last two weeks keeping them up at all hours, screaming and making ridiculous demands. But later, when she calmed down, she realised what she had done was unfair and so made them all a meal by way of apology. She was a good cook and a good person.

Shelly's aggressive behaviour was a result not only of her past, but also her present. While she was suffering from complex post-traumatic stress disorder, she had no space to recover as a result of ongoing abuse. Her boyfriend had taken over the abusive role from her step-father. Shelly was being damaged on a daily basis.

Shelly dominated much of my supervision. I used the extra supervision from my ASYE to frequently reassess the interventions I was using. All my skills were being tested to the extreme. Before working with Shelly, I had no experience of trauma-based social work and I needed to learn more in order to understand the problem I was faced with. Critical reflection was central to the small successes I made with Shelly. Every few weeks I would have more information about Shelly which would lead to a new approach to working with her. Discussing the case with other social workers also meant I did not lose confidence in my abilities. It was therapeutic knowing that I was not totally crap at my job and that the problems I was dealing with did not have a simple answer. The flexibility of my practice, and that of my manager, is, I am sure, the main factor which led to Shelly living with us for the long period that she did.

Eventually, it did come to a point where we could no longer support Shelly effectively. Her risk to staff had become too great. And while Shelly is not yet where she wants to be in life, she did make remarkable progress over the eight months I knew her. Before I met her, Shelly had refused to receive medical attention. After weeks of building up a strong professional relationship, she trusted me enough to register her to a doctor and a psychiatrist. After escorting her to the first few meetings, she eventually began going on her own and continues to receive the treatment she needs. Shelly also learned to budget her money and cook for herself. She can easily manage the practicalities of owning a property. Progress was slow, but the increase in her self-esteem was noticeable. Through long and open conversations with her, Shelly began to realise that she was capable of managing aspects of her life. If she could cook for herself and pay rent, surely she could manage other things, she thought. Every small achievement was an important step in Shelly gaining control over her chaotic life.

THE BENEFITS OF BEING A 'RESCUER'

The benefit of ASYE is that you have to demonstrate your practice. It really makes you conscious of what sort of social worker you want to be, and what values you hold. I was very clear that I wanted to be the social worker who doesn't give up without a fight. I am a sore loser. As a child I was always the banker in Monopoly, and true to life, I took more money for myself when no one was looking to make sure that I could never lose. I realised the degree of my competitiveness when I was still cheating at Monopoly at 21 years of age – subsequently getting into arguments with family members, adamantly denying my cheating. After two hours of shouting, I realised that I needed to get a grip. Monopoly is not worth arguing about. While I have managed to control my competitiveness to some degree, it still rumbles under the surface. This, combined with my tendency to want to 'rescue' young people, makes me a force to be reckoned with sometimes. And there are some things that are definitely worth arguing for two hours about. I despise the saying 'difficult young person'. I want to exhaust all options before saying we cannot support someone anymore. My determination to help Shelly exhausted my manager, but luckily she understood this desire in me and has a heart of pure gold.

I think it's important to say that I am not a perfect social worker, although I'm sure you worked that out by the third page. I have a lot to learn and a lot of flaws. But I am trying, and every NQSW is in the same position. If you think you know it all then I can guarantee that your practice is dangerous. *Wisest is she who knows she does not know.*

11 Conclusion

THE GOOD LIFE IS ONE INSPIRED BY LOVE AND GUIDED BY KNOWLEDGE – BERTRAND RUSSELL

Being in love is a funny thing. The person you're in love with can become a confusing entity. Most of the time they are the person who makes you feel warm and safe and full of life. They are the reason you get up in the morning and with them everything seems to make sense. The other five per cent of the time, they are the one person who makes you convinced that, if really pushed, you could probably commit murder. Especially if they keep laughing at that volume at second-rate comedy on BBC3!

I am in love with social work.

A year after graduating, I am very aware that social work is complex and the more I know, the more I realise the depth of those complexities. I knew when I chose to be a social worker that there were things that would need improving, and I liked the idea of being part of those changes. It's a very good time to be a social worker as the discourse is always around change and improvement. We know that there is too much paperwork; we know that there needs to be more emphasis on the emotional support social workers receive; we know that we need to work more closely and effectively with other agencies in order to keep people safe. There is a clear sense of always needing to better ourselves, and that removes any sense of arrogance among practitioners. So, while there are aspects of the profession that are infuriating, there is definitely an air of hope around.

I have no doubt that over the next decade social work will become more important than ever. As the Welfare State is continuously dismantled around us, more people will feel the crippling effects of poverty and isolation. The amount of national stress and sadness will intensify. Sue Miller, an experienced social worker, says in her book *Death of a social worker* that *whilst social workers continue to manage the unmanageable, people's problems will remain unaddressed* (p. 238). Social work has to be so much more than helping individual cases. We have to stand up for what we believe in. We need a unified and national response to the challenges we face. If you are passionate about helping people, then you have to help improve social work. I have made active decisions to develop my social work career at policy level as well, which is why I stood for election to the Professional Assembly at The College of Social Work. I like the contrast it brings. One day I am sitting around a huge oak conference table, admiring the decor of the ornate London building I am in, discussing the future of my profession, and then the next day I am back at home shifting washing machines up three flights of stairs with a young person. Social work undoubtedly needs improving and needs to re-define the role it plays in solving social problems; if you are part of the social work profession then you yourself are a tool for creating these changes.

IS THE STRESS WORTH IT?

While I was warned that social work would be emotionally challenging, it is not something you can fully comprehend until you experience it for yourself. The heartache and disappointment I experienced while on placement still continues in my current practice. I wish I'd known about the dangers of stress and how to manage it. I have always been a workaholic and so I thought I could not get stressed. Little did I know that stress doesn't have to come from work overload but can come from knowing you do not have the resources to effect the change you want to. That has been the biggest struggle for me. However, I'm sure that if I'd had good strategies in place for managing this from the outset, I wouldn't have suffered the stress I did. Saying that, now that I have experienced extreme stress, I am very good at looking after myself – so maybe it was a necessary lesson for me to learn. Even with the heartache, however, I still believe that social work can truly make a positive difference in people's lives. The point is to not stop fighting.

The best description I have ever read of social workers is by Harry Ferguson. For me it sums up perfectly what we do and why I get up every morning despite the challenges:

> *Every day in this country social workers perform countless acts that make a real difference to the lives of thousands of people. What these social workers do involves kindness, compassion, courage, resilience, cleverness, and extraordinary levels of skill and wisdom. Social workers routinely meet the extraordinarily difficult challenge of having to balance empathy and compassion with exercising power and authority to protect the hurt and the vulnerable. They sit with the troubled in their pain, the sick and the dying and help those who are consumed by the grief of losing loved ones. Social workers are the conscience of the good society. They speak for the poor and dispossessed. They heal. Without social workers it would be impossible to claim that this is what we can call a civilized society.*
> —Professor Harry Ferguson, http://swscmedia.com/2012/04/celebrating-social-work-by-prof-harry-ferguson-for-a-special-evening-with-dr-ferguson-swscmedia-tuesday-24-april-2012-04-24-swscmedia/)

If you are considering becoming a social worker, I hope you make the right choice for you. I think the key is to be completely honest with yourself about your limitations and also loyal to your values. The best social workers I know are always those who won't sacrifice what is right for what is easy.

The little interactions you have with your service users are the life blood of social work. One of the gang members I work with comes in every six weeks with a new pair of trainers. This is a man you cannot get to sit down for more than 30 seconds. When he needs his new pair of Nike trainers re-lacing however, he will happily wait 30 minutes until I'm finished in a meeting to get me to lace them. He's happy to wait because *no one else will do 'em right*. I only agree to lace them if he pays some of his rent arrears *seeing as he could afford new trainers*. We have a little debate about it. He always ends up paying and I always end up lacing his trainers. It never fails to make me smile.

The theme that emerges from the social workers I have met, time and time again is that, yes, the profession is stressful and stress management skills are imperative, but if the values of the field resonate with an individual then it is a worthwhile choice. Most social workers have integrity in their work and a real passion for social justice; something that separates it from other professions where the motivations often seem to be social status, stability or money. The authenticity in the motives of social workers produces a profession that is critical of itself and that changes in new and innovative ways.

But even if these things do resonate with you, social work won't be your perfect job. There is no such thing. Even though it isn't a stale office job, it comes with its own frustrations. What social work *is* about is making small differences to real people every day. Social work will consume you. You will take the sadness and the successes home with you and it will change your view of the world.

So you may ask, is it worth it?

Every second of it.

A man goes out on the beach and sees that it is covered with starfish that have washed up in the tide. A little boy is walking along, picking them up and throwing them back into the water.

What are you doing, son? *the man asks.* You see how many starfish there are? You'll never make a difference.

The boy paused thoughtfully, and picked up another starfish and threw it in the ocean.

It sure made a difference to that one, *he said.*

—N.D. Kristoff and S. Wudunn, *Half The Sky*, p. 50

INDEX